A POW'S MEMOIR
FIRST WORLD

THE LEGACY OF THE GREAT WAR
A Series sponsored by the Historical de la Grande Guerre Péronne-Somme

General Editor
JAY WINTER

Previously published titles in the series

Antoine Prost
IN THE WAKE OF WAR
'Les Anciens Combattants' and French Society

Patrick Fridenson
THE FRENCH HOME FRONT 1914–1918

Stéphane Audoin-Rouzeau
MEN AT WAR 1914–1918

Gerald D. Feldman
ARMY, INDUSTRY, AND LABOR IN GERMANY 1914–1918

Rosa Maria Bracco
MERCHANTS OF HOPE

Adrian Gregory
THE SILENCE OF MEMORY
Armistice Day 1919–1946

Ute Daniel
THE WAR FROM WITHIN
German Working-Class Women in the First World War

Annette Becker
WAR AND FAITH
The Religious Imagination in France, 1914–1930

David W. Lloyd
BATTLEFIELD TOURISM
Pilgrimage and the Commemoration of the Great War
in Britain, Australia and Canada, 1919–1939

Alex King
MEMORIALS OF THE GREAT WAR IN BRITAIN
The Symbolism and Politics of Remembrance

Margaret H. Darrow
FRENCH WOMEN AND THE FIRST WORLD WAR
War Stories of the Home Front

Alon Rachamimov
POWS AND THE GREAT WAR
Captivity on the Eastern Front

Antoine Prost
REPUBLICANS IDENTITIES IN WAR AND PEACE
Representations of France in the Nineteenth and Twentieth Centuries

A POW'S MEMOIR OF THE FIRST WORLD WAR

The Other Ordeal

GEORGE CONNES

Translated by
Marie-Claire Connes Wrage

Edited by
Lois Davis Vines

Oxford ● New York

English edition
First published in 2004 by
Berg
Editorial offices:
1st Floor, Angel Court, 81 St Clements Street, Oxford, OX4 1AW, UK
175 Fifth Avenue, New York, NY 10010, USA

© Georges Connes 2004

Berg is the imprint of Oxford International Publishers Ltd.

Library of Congress Cataloging-in-Publication Data

Connes, G. A. (Georges Auguste), 1890–1974.
[Autre épreuve. English]
   A POW's memoir of the First World War : the other ordeal / Georges
Connes ; translated by Marie-Claire Connes Wrage ; edited by Lois Davis
Vines.—English ed.
      p. cm. — (The legacy of the Great War)
   Includes bibliographical references and index.
   ISBN 1-85973-788-9 (pbk.)
   1. Connes, G. A. (Georges Auguste), 1890–1974. 2. World War, 1914–
1918—Prisoners and prisons, German. 3. Prisoners of war—France—
Biography. 4. Prisoners of war—Germany—Biography. 5. World War,
1914–1918—Personal narratives, French. I. Vines, Lois. II. Title. III.
Series.
   D627.G3C6413 2004
   940.4'7243'092—dc22

2004006121

British Library Cataloguing-in-Publication Data

A catalogue record for this book is available from the British Library.

ISBN 1 85973 738 8 (hardback)
       1 85973 788 9 (paperback)

Typeset by JS Typesetting Ltd, Wellingborough, Northants.
Printed in the United Kingdom by Biddles Ltd, King's Lynn.

www.bergpublishers.com

Contents

Biographical Notes:
Georges Connes

March 31, 1890	Born in Paris.
September 1909	Begins university studies in British and American literature at the *École Normale Supérieure* in Paris; completes studies in 1913.
1913	First trip to the United States; teaches in Edinburgh, Scotland.
August 1914	Passes the *agrégation*; drafted into the French army and trained as an officer.
June 1, 1916	Captured at Douaumont near Verdun and sent to prison camp in Mainz, Germany.
December 7, 1917	Prisoners transferred from Mainz to Strasburg (Brodnica) in eastern Prussia.
November 18, 1918	Armistice is signed.
December 29, 1918	Leaves Poland by ship and returns to France via Denmark.
January 15, 1919	Arrives in Cherbourg.
1919–21	Teaches English in a high school in Marseilles.
1924	Appointed Professor of British and American literature at the University of Dijon.
July 1925	Writes his memoir of prison camp.
1926	Completes his doctoral thesis on H.G. Wells.
1927	Marries Henriette Legouis; son, Pierre, born 1928; daughter, Marie-Claire, born 1933.
1934–35	Visiting Professor of French literature at the University of Buffalo.
1935	Municipal Counselor (Socialist) for Dijon.
September 3, 1939	France declares war on Germany.
June 16, 1940	Connes serves as temporary mayor of Dijon when the city government and many citizens flee as the German Army approaches.

June 25, 1940	Armistice signed between France and Germany.
May 1941	Resigns as mayor when the Vichy government asks for the allegiance of the municipality.
November 1943	Organizes the Committee of Liberation secretly in his home.
January 1944	Arrested on suspicion of Resistance activities; released three months later because the Germans did not know the extent of his involvement.
July 1944	Goes into hiding after learning that the Germans have information about him.
September 1944	Selected Mayor of Dijon by Resistants when Dijon is liberated by Allied Forces.
1945	Retires from politics and returns to university teaching.
1946	Awarded Honorary Doctorate at the Centennial of the University of Buffalo.
1947–48	Visiting professor at the University of Buffalo.
1950	Retires from teaching at the University of Dijon.
1950–74	Continues research and writing (see bibliography).
August 13, 1974	Death of Georges Connes.

Foreword

Pierre Connes*

If there are individuals today who should be discreet, it is the intellectuals. The role they played in this war was terrible and unforgivable. Not only did they do nothing to diminish the mutual incomprehension, but with only a few exceptions, they did everything to worsen it. This was partly their war. They poisoned the minds of thousands with their warmongering ideologies. Certain as they were of their truths, proud and inflexible, they sacrificed millions of young lives to the fantasies of their own creation.

Romain Rolland, Les Précurseurs (p. 323)

With a few exceptions? Here is one more exception, totally forgotten today: Georges Connes (1890–1974). Although his family was from the province of Rouergue, his whole career as Professor of British and American Literature was spent at the University of Dijon. He is the author of literary criticism, translations, and articles about regional history. In the present chronicle, Connes is 'a civilian disguised as a soldier,' as he describes himself.

A student at the *École Normale Supérieure*,[1] Connes took the *agrégation* examination in July 1914. The oral part was cancelled, and many of the young men in his class spent their vacation as soldiers at various battlefields in eastern France. The final episode of these experiences at the front is narrated here, starting in the Verdun region near the village of Douaumont, continuing at the Citadel in Mainz, Germany, then ending at another prison camp in eastern Prussia. The author has chosen not to describe his memories of the trenches. Why did he interrupt the writing of his thesis (a much more urgent task) in the summer of 1925 to produce a memoir

*Pierre Connes is Director of Research at the Centre National de Recherches Scientifiques, and is the son of Georges Connes.

of his captivity, especially since the genre was not particularly rare at the time? Because he suddenly discovered that there was still much left to be said on the subject. His high school classmate Charles Moulié, also a former officer prisoner, had just published his own memoir using the pen-name Thierry Sandre. The book, entitled *Le Purgatoire* (Purgatory) was awarded the Goncourt prize[2] in 1924, which made it well known. Sandre's message is crystal clear: the Germans are uniformly stupid and wicked. Connes's project is an attempt to offer the French a better understanding of the actions, reactions, and psychology of the enemy as seen in one of its least pleasant incarnations, the prison guard. His narrative was obviously a dangerous undertaking at a rather badly chosen moment, when the intellectual climate in France was ultra-nationalistic and strongly anti-German. Connes added this final note to his own manuscript in 1932: 'I wrote this seven years ago; seven publishers have refused it.' Discouraged by the rejections, he seems to have simply set aside his text, which he never even showed to his children. Long after the author's death, the manuscript of *The Other Ordeal* was discovered at the bottom of an old trunk in the attic of the family home in Rouergue and accepted for publication in Paris in 2001. Thierry Feral, director of the collection 'Germany Yesterday and Today' at L'Harmattan press, wrote in his preface to the French edition of Connes's memoir:

> Shortly after 1918, under the pressure of the trauma of war and the constantly growing political tensions, there could obviously not be a 'reasonable' vision of Germans in France. It was a time of hatred. Even the smallest villages, schools and the press fostered the obsession with the *Boche*, the strongly pejorative term for a German perceived as a genetically militaristic, warmongering, expanionistic barbarian. By opposing the attitude current at the time, by rebelling against the warmongers and other French chauvinists, and by stating that Germans too 'are human beings and have a soul,' Professor Connes deserves a prominent place among the pioneers of Franco-German reconciliation.

Is Georges Connes's persistent internationalism, which in 1925 might have been taken for disguised Germanophilia, sufficient to explain the unanimous rejection by publishers in the 1920s? After all, Romain Rolland had been able to publish *Au-dessus de la Mêlée* (Above the Battle), though he did so in Switzerland at first, and had long been recognized as a famous writer.[3] Jean Giraudoux's *Siegfried et le Limousin* had just appeared and received a certain amount of success. Giraudoux's message, barely hidden in the accomplished verbiage, is that the transformation of a Frenchman into a German, during the war or since then, is an easy and reversible procedure; all that is needed is to learn a lesson. Georges Connes's message is essentially the same. But Giraudoux was writing a novel, and readers could enjoy his brilliant style without ever believing in his plot. Connes, on the other hand, was describing actual ordinary experiences in terms that radically contradicted those not just of Sandre, but of many of his peers. According to Connes, German guards were neither deceitful nor cruel by nature, and the prisoners, at least the officers, could hardly complain about the way they were treated.

Another obvious difficulty was, without any doubt, the total absence of fantastic elements, such as the spectacular escapes or other daring acts recounted by former prisoners. Anecdotes of this type fill only one paragraph in Connes's memoir and they are almost all failures. Even worse, the author describes himself as a 'domestic rabbit' who does not try to flee. From his standpoint, why escape? If he had returned to France, what would he have become: 'the killer or the killed'?

Finally, there is only one historical character in the whole narrative, Commanding Officer Raynal, the defender of the Vaux Fort who was captured a few days later than the men in the woods of La Caillette and his role is very limited. As Georges Connes himself remarks in relation to his own memoir, 'nothing happens.' The value of his account lies in its humanistic quality and warmth.

Georges Connes had a profound esteem for Julien Benda, although his memoir precedes by two years Benda's most well-known work, *La Trahison des clercs* (Betrayal of the Intellectuals), whose central theme he anticipates. In his Introduction, Connes is indignant about the attitude of many intellectuals and 'their deliberate and absolute misunderstanding of the foreigner, of the enemy . . . If distinguished intellects function this way, what hope is there for uneducated, ordinary minds?' There is, however, in *The Other Ordeal* a major gap that is rather hard to explain: the absence of any reference to the great European pacifists of the time, such as Stefan Zweig and Romain Rolland. Much later, in 1948, Connes presented and published a lecture on Rolland that reveals his admiration for the French writer and certain parallels in their respective evolutions. Both men were to give up total pacifism during the Second World War.

The Other Ordeal predates by twelve years Jean Renoir's film *The Grand Illusion*, which shed a similar light: the Germans are not horrible creatures! However, the demands of the motion picture industry required a dramatic escape for the denouement. The film was shot at the castle of Haut-Koenigsbourg but it seems probable that Renoir meant to suggest the Citadel at Mainz. Certain scenes showing the camp routine appear to come straight from *The Other Ordeal*. For example, there is a scene showing the opening of packages sent by the families, and another in the mess hall that are very similar to Connes's account. Although anecdotes of this kind were frequent in prisoners' memoirs, what is really remarkable here is the similar state of mind. *The Grand Illusion* was made under the Popular Front, and the French political climate had changed a great deal by then. It seems hard to understand why Georges Connes did not take advantage of this fact to try to publish his memoir during this period.

Thierry Sandre would never have the opportunity to read Connes's 'counter-memoir,' which he had so strongly inspired unknowingly. Yet it is interesting to mention the fate of the two classmates who differed widely in their views and experiences. We are struck by the irony of the final destinies of Connes and Sandre. In 1941, Sandre, a prisoner in Germany for the second time, while at his camp at Munster in Westphalia, wrote a collection of translations of the German press at that time plus an introduction to a few so-called objective notes, which are in reality a typical echo of Vichy literature. His explicit aim is to make the French hear the German refrain that they (the French) are guilty of not admitting responsibility in both wars. At that very moment, Georges Connes, free from German detention but not to remain so for long, was preparing leaflets against collaboration, a newly invented term. The two former classmates actually remained what they had always been, Sandre, a dyed-in-the-wool Germanophobe, Connes, a citizen of the world but not of the Vichy-style 'New Europe.'

Georges Connes's attitude, hard to accept for the vast majority of his compatriots in 1925, will shock only a few today, perhaps. Better still, his narrative deserves to be known in today's Germany, on the condition, however, that its potential readers on both sides of the Rhine know that Connes's fundamental pacifism and internationalism were not to prevent him from joining the French Resistance during the Second World War. A long time after the second war, Georges Connes discovered that his too hasty release from prison in 1944 was due to the intervention of a German professor, an earnest and influential Nazi who nonetheless believed that reconciliation was possible through the intellectuals. It is interesting to imagine that Georges Connes could have written about his second captivity, again limiting himself strictly to personal experience. Although his second narrative might have been as understanding of his guards as the first one, we must not forget the context. After surviving Verdun and German prison camps in the First World War, he was equally lucky twenty-eight years later not to be deported along with several of his fellow Resistants. Would his beliefs have survived? Never in 1944 could he have exchanged a few words with guards at Dora, Dachau or Ravensbrück, and write, as he did in Mainz on Christmas Eve 1916 'after all, they are men and they have souls.' Deportation was quite another ordeal, of which neither Sandre nor Georges Connes could have for one instant imagined the immeasurable horror.

Notes

1. The *École Normale Supérieure* (ENS), a university-level institution in Paris founded in 1794, prepares students for teaching in high schools and universities. The prestigious school has produced numerous scholars, writers, and politicians such as Jean-Paul Sartre, Henri Bergson, Louis Pasteur and Georges Pompidou. Georges Connes graduated first in his class in 1914. The *agrégation* is a highly competitive exam that is required in order to be a high school teacher. About 40 per cent of ENS graduates died in the First World War as compared to 25 per cent as a national average of men in the military.

2. The *Prix Goncourt* is a literary prize awarded annually by the Goncourt Academy, a literary society founded in 1896 by Edmond Goncourt. He and his brother Jules are the authors of naturalistic novels such as *Germinie Lacerteux* (1864) and *Renée Mauperin* (1864).

3. Rolland's theme is summed up in the quotation at the beginning of this Preface. Rolland's pacifism was often misunderstood, and he was accused of being a traitor to his country, although his goal was a search for peace. He was active in the Geneva International Agency for the treatment of prisoners of war.

Introduction

I never thought I would write a memoir about my captivity. Those experiences are already far away, barely surviving except in the minds of individuals who lived through them. The incidents themselves are ordinary. I have long been a little taken aback by the audacity of former prisoners who recounted in detail the little adventures that happened to so many thousands of men as if they were important events. Basically, all prisoners witnessed the same things, minor incidents compared with the realities of war. Only a few have dared to create literary works out of these petty annoyances and the insignificant exchanges of jabs that took place far from the real battlefield. When all is said and done, we must realize that prisoners of war slept inside most nights, away from the risk of mutilation and death, and we had something to put in our bellies almost every day. Being in the habit of only talking about what I know first-hand, I will limit my account to the experiences of the officers, referring only occasionally to the Russian officers, who practically starved to death by the thousands. While not intending to underestimate the moral suffering of prisoners of war (I know that many did not make it back), I remind myself that the proportion of fatalities among prisoners during and after captivity was much smaller than among the men who fought and were not captured. In short, I used to consider, rightly or wrongly, that ex-prisoners should be discrete, even silent, about our suffering out of respect for those who were condemned to continue the battle.

It was in this frame of mind that I read Thierry Sandre's book *Le Purgatoire*, which made me very angry. Before reading this work, I admired him as a talented writer who conscientiously collected the works of young writers killed during the war. When Thierry Sandre was known by his real name, Charles Moulié, he, Marcel Prouille and I were classmates in high school and enjoyed writing rhymed verse and other 'poetic' diversions while pretending to listen to a philosophy teacher, no doubt a genius but incomprehensible to us.[1] Already

1

at that time, Moulié had a deep scorn for teachers, whom he considered to be people who do nothing but chew over others' thoughts. Even then, Moulié's determination to become a writer was stronger than I have ever seen in a young man. His literary career, which would include poetry, novels, and translations, seemed as clearly laid out as my own ambition to earn advanced degrees and eventually be awarded a university professorship at a provincial institution. Moulié probably even envisioned winning the Goncourt literary prize at some point. I sometimes wonder if this is how great writers are made.

Thierry was, to my mind, an excellent classmate whose intellect I admired in those early days, which makes me all the more upset that he wrote such a pernicious book. It is a shame that the Goncourt Academy has chosen to honor his book along with others he has written with an award. But it is too bad only for Thierry Sandre. The Goncourt Academy, which selected *Le Feu* for a prize, is above suspicion of being nationalistic.[2] Thierry Sandre wrote better works than *Le Purgatoire*. To begin with, the title is rather pretentious because it would appear that we, who went through the experience of captivity, have the right to call the misfortunes of this world unfair and that we have the right to enter paradise directly. The title is a confession, even if it is not what Sandre intended. It was *only* purgatory; hell was elsewhere.

I am convinced Sandre's book is dangerous because it is overtly filled with hatred. It always makes me angry when I encounter a decent individual trapped in the eternal illusion that the national group into which one happens to be born holds the monopoly of virtue and that other groups or nationalities are intrinsically evil. The misunderstanding of the foreigner, of the enemy if you like, is deliberate and absolute in Sandre's book. If distinguished intellects function this way, what hope is there for the uneducated, ordinary minds?[3] Perhaps we can expect more after all. The normal and natural attitude is total indifference toward individuals who live out of sight, on the other side of the mountain, so to speak. Put quite simply, human beings are capable of hatred toward others in reverse proportion to how much one is exposed to the media or to the bellicose literature that Thierry Sandre feeds on. He has not gotten over the psychosis of 1916; even worse, there are no signs of improvement in him. I particularly resent his stating that in 1924 he would make no changes in what he wrote in 1916. He has no doubts about the 'truths' he expressed in 1916, when he stated 'others are coming back howling, wounded men. For Germans who suffer cry out.' Of course, Frenchmen suffer in silence. Sandre observes that 'Germans have a special odor.'[4] How I would love to place Sandre in front of six naked men and ask him to identify the Germans among them by their smell. Sandre is unable to recognize even one hint of kindness or humanity in a German. Every time the author mentions a German throughout his account of captivity, he quickly uncovers the calculations behind the apparent generosity of his captors. I find his shrewdness rather frightening. How could he not have realized, like everyone else, that hatred for the enemy increased gradually as one went farther away from the front? Sandre admits to the fraternal feelings among the combatants, who were enemies shortly before but now join together to partake of a loaf of bread and a cup of coffee. Right away, Sandre is suspicious of the system, of Germany's intention of creating an illusion about its food supplies. The author reports that he asked some poor fellows the 'serious' question: 'Are prisoner officers allowed to keep on being served by their orderlies?' and the Germans usually answered yes, obviously without knowing anything about it. What would Sandre have answered if a German officer had asked him the same question? As for myself, I do not know even today. The questions asked by combatants about the routine for prisoners were futile; nobody ever knew what went on in the camps, except the prisoners and the guards. But Sandre imagines a vast conspiracy of deceit: the Germans always promised and never kept their word. The officer who agreed to pass on a letter to the prisoner's wife lied; the colonel who promised a decent burial for someone lied . . . probably. Thierry Sandre does not have any proof. But what else can one expect from a German? According to Sandre, 'It is certain that Germans are born deceitful, treacherous by nature and vile in all respects.' As everyone knows, the French are, on the contrary, born honest, loyal by nature, and noble in all endeavors. He continues:

> And let no one tell us that this brutish and conniving Germany is the creation of a Kaiser, dynasty or caste. We, prisoners who have suffered at the hands of Germans during every moment of our captivity, we know that the most modest peasant in Saxony, the humblest Bavarian factory worker, and the lowest-level merchant in Hanover are, equally with the highest Prussian landowners, cruel men, dishonorable, jealous and inhumane; they all have the souls of executioners, if they have souls.

As is well known, on the contrary, the most modest peasant in Beauce, the humblest factory worker in Puteaux and the ordinary business employee in Le Havre[5] have souls characterized by sublime nobleness and infinite generosity almost equal to Renan and Anatole France.[6] Sandre dares to add: 'I am expressing myself here without any passion, I swear.' Should we laugh? Should we cry? Those of us who still have some hope for the nasty beast we call the human being should cry.

I am far from denying totally the value of Sandre's approach. He shows in a rather plausible manner, already known before him, that much earlier and much more systematically than that of other countries Germany's treatment of prisoners was inspired by organized methods and designed to influence the morale of enemy populations. But the curious thing is that Sandre seems to be blaming Germany for the system, as if the process were illegitimate, while at the same time deploring our own slowness in doing the same. What we have here, basically, is the old, naive idea according to which the ignominy of war should be carried out according to certain rules, duly agreed upon and classified. The classic formula so readily used by the Germans to take care of all recriminations, those of their prisoners, their troops, their population, the answer to everything, 'this is war,' was their ultimate response to all situations and their final truth. The prisoners, Sandre seems to be saying, felt that for them at least, there should not have been war anymore, and that because of their captivity they should automatically have been placed outside the fray. As for myself, disarmed and powerless after the merciless fury of the battlefield, I was constantly amazed that I had not been knocked senseless or thrown into some jail cell to survive on bread and water.

I am going to say something that might be considered shocking: if by our own choice and use of means to kill, we have been more monstrous in this war than ever before, the horror of the treatment of prisoners is far from having increased proportionately, and I am not at all certain that such treatment has not been better than ever, given the enormous number of prisoners.[7]

It is certainly very easy to show that Germany's policy concerning the treatment of prisoners evolved as the war progressed toward the final demise. The Germans became tougher on the captives when defeat was probable. Our astute psychologists assure us that this attitude is a purely German character trait. Personally, I think it is purely human. Individuals or nations when fighting for survival are all the more gentle when they are more certain of victory; conversely, they are more brutal when certain of defeat. One should, at least, study the documents and hear the impressions of the other side. Perhaps one should not forget that the Allied Forces showed their 'magnanimity' by keeping their prisoners for a year and a half after the war ended. I, myself, believe that prisoners were treated, quite simply, according to the material and moral situations of the countries that held them. In Germany, the prisoners were fed quite decently and handled somewhat roughly as long as Germany had supplies and the hope for victory. They were fed less well and handled more roughly gradually as supplies and hope diminished. In the Allied camp, where famine was less of a threat, the food supply varied less, but the discipline became more and more severe. As for the cases of brutality quoted by Sandre, second-hand, they all date back to August or at the latest to September 1914, when the rage of war was at its climax in a Germany athirst for victory. Everyone knows that a crowd, nationalistic or otherwise, is a rather vile thing in any country. I would really like to know if all German prisoners taken by the Allied Forces at that time have had nothing but compliments for the manner in which they were treated; and as soon as one refers to specific examples, one's case is lost.

Sandre's book lacks measure, fairness, and humanity. Before reading it, I thought there could only be too many books written by prisoners; now I am convinced that there will never be enough books on the subject. More are needed, written by men of all opinions and feelings, but who will never forget this essential fact: 'It was war.' Any account of individual humiliations or suffering not placed in the context of this general phenomenon so that its exact measure can be taken seems, to my mind, without value. The general history of the prisoners of The Great War has not yet, to my knowledge, been written and particularly that of the two or three million men who ended up crowded into camps of a famished and harassed Germany, which had to incarcerate and feed them. There are Germans who think that these prisoners were the cause of their country's downfall. For the historians who will undertake this great task, many books will be necessary. They must not all be like Sandre's.

The personality of the man writing the present memoir is of little importance. My book is written not so much by a man as by a state of mind, the state of mind of those for whom appearances were not enough, and for whom visceral resentment to suffering or constraint was not the only possible reaction. I hope this book is perceptive and honest. If I did not write it, others would. I expect that others are writing it along with me.

Captivity was *the other ordeal*. The major ordeal, of course, was that of the fighting, mud and blood. I am sorry for those who, from either ordeal, returned having forgotten nothing or learned nothing. But it was in the other ordeal, in the prisoner of war camps, that we could learn, if we did not already know it, that a man is a man and nothing more. Nothing very admirable, whatever the color or shape of his clothes or the language he speaks. I am also still simple-minded enough to feel some anger against those who have not learned this basic truth.

I believe that the Hohenzollern were the main culprits and that their disappearance is a good thing for Germany and for the world.[8]

I hardly think I will be accused of being a German agent. I am quite resigned to being called naive.

Notes

1. Marcel Prouille, using the pseudonym Marcel Ormoy, published a few collections of poems between 1910 and 1913 in periodicals such as *Pantagruel* and *Chloé*.

2. *Le Feu, Journal d'une Escouade* (Under Fire, the Story of a Squad) by Henri Barbusse first appeared in installments in *L'Oeuvre* (August 1916), then was published by Flammarion (November 1916). It immediately received the Goncourt Prize. Georges Connes did not learn about the book until after the war. The book evokes the grim and horrific everyday life from the point of view of the common soldier.

3. Visiting a Russian prisoners' camp, talking both about the prisoners and their Austrian guards, Stefan Zweig writes 'these simple and primitive men had a much more just feeling about the war than our poets and university professors . . . each one of whom had been involved in this tragedy was somehow a brother' (*The World of Yesterday*, p. 242).

4. Sandre is not alone in thinking that the Germans have a particular smell. Thoughts on this subject were formulated in 1917 by a professor of medicine and published by the French Association for the Advancement of Science and quoted by Annette Becker in *Oubliés de la grande guerre* (p. 328). The whole chapter 'A biological conception of characteristics' illustrates very well the attitude that Georges Connes is trying to refute.

5. Saxony, Bavaria, and Hanover are German provinces. Beauce is a province south-west of Paris. Puteaux is a working-class suburb west of Paris. Le Havre is an important Atlantic harbor located at the estuary of the Seine river.

6. Ernest Renan (1823–92) is the author of *Avenir de la Science* (The Future of Science) (1890), which demonstrates his faith in science and his disaffection with religion based on historical and linguistic research. Anatole France (1844–1924) wrote novels expressing ironic skepticism and a humanistic attitude such as those found in *Histoire contemporaine* (Contemporary History) (1899–1901).

7. Romain Rolland writes in *Au-dessus de la Mêlée*: 'The war, which reached a level of cruelty far beyond what previous wars in the Western Hemisphere led to imagine is, in contrast, less hard for all those (be they wounded or prisoners) who have been withdrawn from the action itself' (p. 61). Rolland, who worked for a long time at the International Agency for Prisoners in Geneva, notes:

> The letters that we receive [from Germany] show that the Germans are trying to reconcile humanitarianism with the demands of war, that there is no difference between the care given to the Germans wounded and the Allied wounded, that friendly relations are established between the prisoners and their guards, and that food is the same for both groups. I wish that a similar inquiry would be made and published about the German prisoners' camps in France (pp. 61-2).

8. The Hohenzollern were a German royal family that included rulers of Brandenburg (1415-1918), Prussia (1701-1918) and Germany (1871-1918).

1

From Verdun to Mainz

On the slopes of the forest of La Caillette, on June 1, 1916, Schneider and I once again resurfaced from under the heaps of earth that had buried us many times for the past two days.[1] The moment we emerged, a Bavarian soldier, swinging a grenade above our heads, shouted '*Raus! Raus!*' (out! out!) What could we do? We came out, looking like miners who had just been extracted from under a rockslide and seemed to be still in shape to fight. We were beginning to get used to being buried that way. Interment is better than being torn apart and proves that the shell fell far enough away so that we simply nestled in one of the sides of the crater. If one is not buried too deeply, if the weight of the earth on the back and legs is not too great, and if one can breathe a little, the situation can even become rather pleasant, in comparison with what is going on outside. One can, with some calm effort, even experience a feeling of security similar to the ostrich that sticks its head in the sand. I confess that during one of my temporary burials, I tried to persuade myself that by remaining under my blanket of dirt, I was less at risk of being annihilated by my fellow humans. On previous occasions, when we had finally come out from our earth tomb, we anxiously searched the horizon in the direction of Douaumont wondering: Are they coming? They hadn't come yet.[2] But this time they did come and so efficiently that their first line passed over us without our being aware of anything. They were already climbing up the slopes of Souville, almost a mile behind us.[3] The man with the grenade was one of those who followed at a distance to make a clean sweep of the area.

Still today, the man with the grenade appears magnanimous to me; he didn't throw it. Obviously, it was not necessary to drop a grenade at that point, but it would have been quite easy and must have been very tempting. Bavarian friend, you were neither a coward nor a butcher. Had I been you, would I have had your self-control and your calm judgment? Perhaps he was thinking 'These enemy soldiers emerging from the ground are apparently disarmed, but could a

9

deadly shot come from one of them?' Mulot, a second lieutenant in the 171st Regiment, who was either an electrical or civil engineer in eastern France, has often told me a story about what happened to him early one morning. Taken by surprise and overpowered quickly by a few soldiers, he handed over the revolver he carried as an orderly, then changed his mind, pulled a Browning out of his pocket, and fired at the young German doctor in the artillery group, breaking his jaw. This act is undeniable treachery and should have ended in instant death, right? But with a motion of his hand, the wounded man stopped the other Germans from firing and gave Mulot his card, saying: 'After the war is over, come see me in Koenigsberg.' Thierry Sandre will say that he wanted to prove that Germans are not barbarians. Bavarian friend, if you are still alive, wherever you are, whoever you are, I would like to shake the hand that did not kill me when it could have, an act that would only have been an insignificant and common incident on the battlefield.

The man with the grenade makes a gesture to indicate the direction we must follow, pointing to the fort at the top of the slope we were climbing. I don't linger. French shells are starting to reach the area. What a sad end to be killed by friendly fire. I give up the idea that came to me briefly of trying to dig out my buried knapsack, in which I had some rations. Since one of my leggings won't stay on, I abandon the other one too. In a crazy impulse, I gulp down the rest of a flask of mint spirits found in my pocket. With my clothes, my helmet and a blanket as my sole worldly possessions, I take off toward Douaumont, running the most terrible race of my life. I don't wait for Schneider, who is fat. I am lean. He can't keep up with me, and I don't see any advantage to him in both of us being torn to shreds by the same shell.

The shelling of a ground position by heavy artillery is not as terrible as one might think. It 'only' kills three quarters of those exposed to it. In a little while, I will see thirty-two or thirty-three men still alive from my company. Three days ago there were 110 of us. Along with Schneider and a few others, I thought we were the only survivors of this non-stop shelling, but now I see, here and there, alone or in small groups, men in blue uniforms running and climbing the slope like me, each according to his strength, until exhaustion. A little to my right, a sergeant is killed on the spot by shrapnel from a 75-millimeter piece of artillery. A man falls, mutilated, screaming. For a moment, a group of backup German machine-gunners, squatting on standby, point their guns at me as I am climbing toward them. They save a few cartridges that would be so easy to spend for my benefit. I walk by without them even looking at me. Machine-gunners, thank you. Ready to faint, as I have never felt after physical effort, I finally plunge into one of the corridors of Fort Douaumont, which was still undamaged at that time and even remains so today. My fellow survivors and I collapse on the ground in the dark, ready to die. That mint alcohol has killed me. I throw up, feeling as if I am going to retch what is left of my life along with it. People believe that I am wounded; they step away from me. A German officer looks at me for an instant with military correctness and even, possibly, a glimmer of sympathy. It's over. I get up again and go join the crowd of soldiers.

We take a short break to wait for our comrades in blue uniforms – bruised, muddy, bloody – and a few armed German soldiers to catch up. Schneider arrives a long time after me, finally ending his climb safely. Other comrades are here too, among them little Felix, who last night, after a violent shelling, had gone down to the first-aid station. I say first-aid station but that is a joke for it is in reality a sort of hole in a hollow where they pile up the wounded without being able to give them any care. The station has been overrun by the enemy, and the wounded who can't walk are still there, waiting to be crushed to death. I move toward my two buddies, saying 'Well, the Krauts got us!' (In those days, I spoke like everyone else.) A furious voice explodes near me: '*Nicht Schimpfen!*' (no insults!) I slink away into the dark thinking 'Aren't they going to kill me on the spot?'

A movement is felt in this pitiful crowd. We advance toward the end of the corridor, go down some stairs that plunge into darkness, where we have to proceed single file. I am seized by a terrifying thought: Aren't we going to be shot right there? Isn't some executioner waiting for us at the bottom, ready for us to file past his bayonet, his revolver or his machine gun, like pigs in a Chicago slaughter house under the killer's mallet? Or perhaps like in a movie I saw recently in which the soldiers were filing through a postern gate under Robin Hood's hatchet? This is how men were made to think about one another in 1916; they thought that was how prisoners were treated. At the end of the dark staircase, there is nothing but another gallery, at the end of which we can see daylight. We soon come out of the tunnel and exit on the north side of Douaumont.[4]

Frantic running starts again, still under French shells. The goal for our leaders and ourselves is to get out of their range as fast as possible. For now, we are led, meaning that here and there, interspersed among us, are some German soldiers who have appeared out of nowhere. As for me, I am following a little man with glasses who looks like a clothing salesman, obviously one of those soulless executioners Thierry Sandre will talk about. Another Frenchman is killed right in front of me as we are running down the infernal gravel-covered ravines. Gradually, as we are coming out of the shelled area, we slow down and end up walking. It is high time, as I am at the end of my strength. Then comes the nervous tension, the horrible exhaustion I am beginning to feel all over my body, the thirst that is beginning to consume me. Never again will I be as thirsty and never will I drink as many liters of water from every ditch as I do on that day, June 1, 1916. All these feelings finally overcome the anxiety caused by the overwhelming need to react and to escape death. I suddenly feel a furious rage at being defeated and being nothing more than an object ordered about. For a long time I have had no illusions about the gestures I make in this absurd human conflict, yet I feel a deep resentment at being no more than an animal in a herd that has been captured by the other side. Like all men, I could count on the fingers of one hand the times I have cried since becoming a man. On that day, I cried, from anger as much as from exhaustion, while following the little Bavarian soldier with the glasses.

We finally reach headquarters, where the highest-ranking officer seems to be an artillery major. They invite the officers in and offer us cigars and coffee, that is to say the liquid bearing that name during the war, and nobody refuses. Thierry Sandre doesn't seem to have refused either. Without bragging, the German officers show us on the map the terrain they have gained by the attack. They don't ask us any naive questions such as 'Do you think we will take Verdun?' or 'When will the war be over?' These men seem to be educated, serious, and without illusions. As on our side, stupidity and bragging will increase gradually as one goes back behind the lines. It is barely 6 a.m., June 1 and it is already known here that yesterday in the North Sea, 'the German fleet destroyed the British fleet.'[5] We suspect that this bit of news will need some clarification. In fact, at the precise moment the officers are talking to us, the German battleships are already steaming away at full speed toward their home ports, if they haven't already reached them, never to leave again until surrender.

For a few minutes, there is a break in the turmoil, and we can begin to think. Then suddenly outside, very close by, tremendous explosions from the French 155-millimeter shells shake the ground. Hearing shouts in the distance, a young medic goes outside. He returns after a while looking very pale. A shell has fallen right in the middle of a reserve company, which a short while ago had sneered a little as we walked by them. Fifty men lie there, either dead or wounded. It's our turn to sneer a bit, more or less openly. I am not unhappy about this.

When the shelling lets up, they start us walking again, indicating for us to follow a general direction heading north, climbing slopes, then crossing a wide plateau. We move along in small groups freely constituted, walking and stopping as we like, as if we are a bunch of tourists on a hike. Where to? One of the few German soldiers who seem to be taking a walk with us has a vague answer: 'To division headquarters.' Nothing would be easier at that moment than to escape, to stop, hide in some hole or behind a rock, wait for night and try to rejoin the French lines, which are at most a few kilometers away. Prisoners have done that sometimes, because they have had the strength to do it. None of us has enough energy left. Even those for whom escape will soon become an obsession won't attempt anything today while it's easy and success reasonably probable. The fact is we have reached the extreme limits of exhaustion. Escape is not an option. We need to drop right here on the spot, sleep for twenty-four hours, then spend another three days eating and sleeping, but we must walk on. We are starving, the sun is fierce, and there is not a scrap to eat nor a drop to drink. I don't have a penny in my pocket, and my billfold is buried in one of my knapsacks. Big Schneider, absolutely worn out, is dragging behind. I grab one of his arms and help him along as best I can in my state. His other hand holds onto a stick. This sturdy, 200-pound fellow is shuffling along as if he had suddenly turned into an old man. Let me use this remarkably new simile and say that my whole body feels as if it has been beaten all over. I am beginning to have feverish visions of the food rations I left behind when I decided that life came first. And then, all of a sudden, while I am climbing up the road of my Calvary, an inner joy springs forth in me. It grows, blooms, and completely overwhelms me: Idiot, you were crying just now? I welcome June 1, 1916, the most beautiful day of my life! I won't die, I won't be killed anymore; I have totally done my duty toward my countrymen, I have not tried to escape from it, and death has passed me by. I will not be that last guy I just passed, whose head is crushed, whose body is turned inside out like an empty puppet. I almost became that victim at twenty-six and I know that now I won't. How could one expect that my soul wouldn't be flooded with joy in my broken body? Sunlight, cool water, ripe fruit, women's soft skin, all of which I have stupidly enjoyed so little until now, at this instant I sign a new lease with you that must endure for fifty years, at least.

Meanwhile, I have to keep following the pathetic column northward. During one of our halts, a German artilleryman, who came out of a nearby wood where his battery is positioned, approaches us. He wants to talk. Before the war, he worked as a grocery boy in Neuilly.[6] Right away I dislike him; he boasts, lies, is full of insinuations and official optimism: the fall of Verdun is near and the course of the war hinges on it. We Frenchmen have too much good sense to have a discussion with him and we barely answer. He appears to understand this, for he suddenly walks away without saying good-bye, waiting for a better chance to express his useless sentiments. The area seems surprisingly empty of troops and equipment. Apparently, there are not even any organized retreat positions. Are the Germans already removing the bulk of their forces in order to direct them toward the region where they expect our next offensive? On our left, however, there are some long-range guns mounted on rails that are not shooting. Are they the 420-millimeter cannons? Then, almost immediately, we see the division. According to the German bulletin, there are too many of us to be personally interviewed by high-placed people. If my memory is correct, there were seventy-five officers and 2,000 enlisted men captured during this operation. In the open air, we are subjected to the first series of procedures designed to transform us rapidly from men into prisoners, from individuals into numbers, more or less. Up until now, we were merely combatants who had unfortunately been overtaken by the first enemy line, just about forgotten and roaming around on the battlefield. The Germans were hardly aware of us anymore, just as a chess player doesn't think about the pawns he has already won and casually set aside. It seemed that all they wanted was for us to get out of the way fast. Now we are falling into the cogs of the infernal machine prepared for us.

The machine, so close to the front, is still functioning rather poorly. It is obvious that, except for the general instructions and the gathering points, nothing is clearly defined. First we, the officers, are separated from the French soldiers, whom we will not see again. The question of the orderlies, which worried Thierry Sandre so much, does not even come up for us. An officer is an officer, a soldier, a soldier. The moment of saying good-bye to our men is heart-breaking. There are tears on several faces of the men and the officers. Friends, when will we see one another again? Maybe never. Most often it has been never. The Germans simply have us pass in front of a portable table, behind which sit an officer and several warrant officers, and we are invited to empty our pockets. Weapons, maps, and compasses, considered war spoils, are confiscated, as we are clearly informed. Our personal papers and letters are collected in packages with our names on them and will, they say, be sent back to us after inspection. We get to keep as our own property objects of personal use, including food items and money. Such are the rules we are informed about, and we are trusted to follow them. No violence is inflicted on anyone, no pocket searched, no insult uttered. In fact, everyone can keep hiding what he wants and besides, everyone destroyed long ago anything that might reveal any information to the enemy. But surely they in the division are not worried for they know that whatever might escape this casual search, meant mostly to gather information of urgent concern, will not escape the net that is set for us further on as we approach the rear.

It is impossible for me to hide the fact that we are still waiting for those packages of letters and papers they were supposed to send us in our camps. Some prisoners were, are, and will be very indignant about it, but I am not. This is war. We are in the middle of the storm, barely out of range of the heavy artillery, and the greatest battle of all time is being waged. It is obvious there is not time to waste. Can one start debating with each prisoner to persuade him to turn over the documents, handwritten or printed, that he has in his pocket? Dealing with the French, eternally argumentative and prone to protest, would take too much time. A little official lie is so much easier; it obviously seems to be the expedient thing to do for those who tell it, mechanically, for the hundredth time. The Germans know they will have more important concerns than packing and mailing hundreds of old papers to the 'Gentleman Prisoners.' The Germans are still in the heat of battle and can't be very impressed by the fondness for these old things shown by those who are no longer in danger. They are not entirely wrong. I myself confess that I have totally forgotten what I might have left in their hands. Someone will probably say that I'm excusing lying; I am not excusing it. I am trying to understand it. Everyone knows that in France no one ever lied to the German prisoners, right?

This procedure over, we start northward again, but his time we are more grouped and watched. Now we can no longer run away without being shot point-blank. We are becoming more and more prisoners of war. Just when we think we are incapable of going any farther, we walk more kilometers. I don't even know how many. Food is out of the question, but we avidly gulp down water under the torrid sun every time we find some and whatever its condition. Those who have something to eat, partake; those who don't are left without. I wouldn't have anything if Felix and Schneider – who is feeling better – didn't share some chocolate and biscuits with me. The day is almost over when we finally reach a village that serves as a first depot. There is, of course, no civilian population. I believe it must be Azanne.[7] We catch a glimpse of a barbed wire enclosure surrounding men in blue coats sprawled directly on the ground with no shelter of any kind. Be we are forced to go in another direction, then enter a house, climb stairs (or rather a short ladder), and enter an attic, where we are locked in. Indeed, we are now literally prisoners.

We collapse on the straw mattresses, which are the only furniture, and hours pass before anything happens or anyone says anything. We only exchange a few vague words, and, for the first time, we are overwhelmed by the horror of our situation. From time to time, the door opens for some newcomers, some of whom we recognize, others we don't. Finally, there are twenty-five or thirty of us. Conversations begin. Our minds are still much more preoccupied with the battle that is ending than with the beginning of our captivity. We are most worried about friends and the overall situation. We don't have the strength to face tomorrow and don't give any thought yet to our future. A totally ordinary German soldier is our only link with the outside world. From the mess hall he brings back, at reasonable prices, decent food in sufficient amounts for those who have money or for those with friends who lend them money, and everyone finds such friends. We are still so close to the front! The fraternity of the trenches hasn't yet become an empty word. Only later in captivity the selfishness of the least generous will awaken little by little, without, however, the generosity of the combatants ever completely dying out.

Another character appears on the scene, a non-commissioned officer who speaks French relatively well and who comes to make the classic speeches that Sandre describes so well: England alone is responsible for the war and its continuation. She will fight to the last Frenchman. Haven't I heard the same thing said by many Frenchmen?

And we will become England's dependents and her colony, slaves to the Anglo-Saxon gold. Even now, in 1925, don't I read everyday in some French newspaper or other that that is indeed what has happened to us? Is it this simple soldier's own idea to come and lecture us? Is he reciting the lesson he has learned and been told to teach us in turn? I believe it is both. He is repeating a lesson but he believes in it, as do all those who repeat it. I can't understand why people are surprised to find that all the Germans they encounter are of an opinion that is merely the reflection of the same official publications. To listen to them, one would think that only Berlin has been engaged in brainwashing. Demartial's book is a testimony to the fact that none of the belligerents has voluntarily renounced this indispensable means of action.[8] What else were the propaganda services doing everywhere? A German prisoner is no doubt informed by the boastful statements of his guards about the wonders of turpinite, the workings of the 'steamroller,'[9] the approaching landing of Russian or Japanese armies, the fact that the army of English athletes was joining the fight, the pending famine and lack of metals in Germany, the decisive intervention of America. Couldn't such a prisoner, provided he had some finesse, recognize here the manipulation of gullible minds by a deceitful press and the hidden persuaders of public opinion? Isn't public policy, everywhere and always, essentially a matter of creating public opinion? In 1925, aren't Paris, Berlin, London and Moscow manipulating opinion? Don't respectable people in 1925 swear by the opinions of Paris, Berlin, London, or Moscow, which they honestly believe to be their own? A man with a personal opinion in 1916 was a rare individual. This is still the case in 1925, and I wonder if evil doesn't begin when this person tries to convert another. Perhaps evil begins when both agree.

Is there among us, in this attic at Azanne, a mole or perhaps several? Maybe you don't know what a mole is. It's a fake prisoner charged with worming information out of the real prisoners. Here are soldiers or officers recently captured, still muddy and bloody from the battlefield. They are locked up, as we are, in their first cell, and, after a moment, someone is brought in who is ostensibly one of their compatriots, obviously muddy and bloody from the same battlefield. Who would suspect anything? Who wouldn't enter into a trusting conversation? This kind of thing is practiced more easily with privates, who are less experienced, or with officers who have been captured alone or in small numbers. Here, today, there are too many of us. Every man knows people in other units, and the mole would soon be discovered. As is well known, the mole is a bastard who deserves to be bled like a pig when he takes advantage of us for the benefit of the enemy. But, on the other hand, he is a hero for whom no reward is too high when he does the same thing among our prisoners for our benefit.

They have brought us our first official prisoner's meal, a thick, unidentifiable mush that seems to be made up of potatoes and semolina but is less disgusting than some mixtures we will encounter later on. Some of us, our stomachs shrunken by days of hunger, fever and nausea or already loaded with nondescript Norwegian sardines, nameless cheese, and generic beer from the canteen, are unable to eat the grub; others, however, gorge on it. How long are we going to stay here? The soldier who is serving us says that we may get going at any moment. Where to? Stenay.[10] On foot? On foot. We are appalled. Stenay is about thirty kilometers away. Exhausted as we are, we'll die on the way. Commanding Officer Mercier swears that we will not go; they will have to provide some means of transport. He has a theory. With the 'Krauts' if you speak loudly, shout vociferously, rant and rage you will win your case. At nightfall, we are barely dozing off in a sleep half-filled, for some, with delirious visions, when the door of the attic opens violently and a voice tells us to get going: '*Sie fahren weiter!*' (You are continuing on your way!) Our preparations don't take long, since, alas, we barely have anything but ourselves to get ready. We go down the ladder staircase and are soon outside. I haven't had a chance until now to say that the gunfire from Verdun is, of course, rumbling non-stop; searchlights are trying to spot airplanes. We are not leaving yet. Commanding Officer Mercier is keeping his word. Without being violent, moreover, but speaking firmly, he states to the German officer in charge of our departure that we are too tired to walk all night. He further argues that the French transport German officer-prisoners by car (How does he know that?) and we demand the same treatment. His request is immediately fulfilled. Within half an hour, five or six peasant carts arrive, each one led by a soldier, and we board in small groups as we like. We are escorted by a few cavalrymen, whom we can barely make out in the dark. This is how we go from Azanne to Stenay. Commander Mercier sees in his success the first proof of his theory: surely, without his intervention, we would have had to walk. Personally, I believe that the German officer from whom we requested something reasonable and easy didn't see any reason to refuse. As for the privates, they will walk the thirty kilometers; no carts for them.

I am not certain, by the way, that walking would have been much worse than being jostled about in the carts. With the horses moving at a walk, it takes us five or six hours to get to Stenay. Their slow gait is a blessing; if they trotted, we would end up dismembered. I am no writer and have already used the meager stock of images and comparisons I had at my disposal to try to express our fatigue. Yesterday and last night on our straw mattresses we thought we were tired. We were in top form compared with how we feel today. Little Felix and I are sitting on the only seat, next to the driver, with whom we don't exchange a single word. Felix is asleep, slumped against me. As I am a little less worn out than he is, I hold him with one arm so that the jolts won't knock him over. Our other comrades, squatting directly on the floor of the cart, look like ghastly cadavers in the pale first light of dawn. The cavalryman who is riding along with us, a lanky, bony, immense fellow, is singing, or rather, humming. What is he singing? I haven't heard German spoken around me again long enough to grasp instantly the meaning of the song.[11] However, I feel that it is hostile and malicious, like the singer himself. It's a war song that is merciless for the traditional enemy.

I no longer think I'm in a peasant's cart. I feel like I'm in a wagon used to haul the condemned to the scaffold. *Uhlan*, a vision from 1870, an image that came to me when I was a little boy, you are like the ones I saw in September 1914 after the battle of the Marne, along the ridges with their lances poised across their saddles like crosses against the sky.[12] You are the same Prussian as the one that old Bélisaire, in Daudet's short story, is waiting for, hidden by the side of the sunken road, ready to let loose on him a swarm of wild bees by poking a stick in their nest.[13] You are the Prussian, the 'Prusco,' as we used to say as children, a term still used at the beginning of the war before we invented 'Boche.' Come on, I think I am a little delirious too, but that's rather normal. You are nothing but an old fool like me whom they have brainwashed while they didn't brainwash me, and who is caught in the infernal machine they have created to persuade us that it is natural, unavoidable, necessary and glorious to make war.

Stenay, at last! A small town like all small French towns. It's a strange sensation, one we are not used to yet, seeing only a few German soldiers walking about there. It is still so early that we see none of the locals. The discrepancy shocks the eye; the Germans in Stenay are already a mistake, an artistic mistake. The French in Mainz and elsewhere in Germany are also an artistic mistake. We are happy, however, that these few foreign soldiers are the only witnesses to our shame. The barracks are like all barracks; they used to house the infantry regiment that was stationed here. One of us served here. It is encircled with barbed wire now with sentries patrolling the perimeter. They drop us off at the door of the main building, have us go up to the fifth floor, and into a room like all barrack rooms. A fifth floor seems like nothing much, yet these four successive flights of stairs were the worst torture inflicted on me in Germany. Of course, we had to go up and down them several times a day to go to the latrines, typical of all French latrines. I always went down and especially up bent double, clinging to the handrail like an old man, step by step. The maneuver takes a good ten minutes going down and fifteen going up. Definitely the clearest consequence of temporary burial by a high-powered explosive is stiffness of the body; that's a fact. When we leave here on June 6 – today is the 2nd – I will only be starting to feel less tired and stiff. My engine will have a little oil again. It's certainly not our present daily fare that accomplishes this. Everyday at noon they bring us some grub – no other word for it will do – in slop pails. There are not enough plates and metal spoons, so some have to wait until the others have finished eating. When we ask for more plates and spoons, we are told there aren't any. With some goodwill on everyone's part, things finally work out. In the evening, they bring us 'coffee' and 'bread.' For those with money, the canteen offers the same mediocre products as in Azanne.

There I spend four dismal days, the most sinister of my captivity. The joy of knowing that we won't be killed doesn't sustain us for very long, especially when the body is beaten and the soul, consequently, wiped out. Yesterday, we thought that our lives having now been saved, nothing would matter or bother us anymore. One soon gets used to no longer dying. Today, we have almost forgotten about that great joy, life, and we only think about minor things. The heat is atrocious under this roof. By the way, why did they house us so high? It seems to me there is nothing or not much on the floors below. The privates are in other buildings, each one surrounded, like ours, with barbed wire inside the general enclosure. The barrack room gives us a preview of all the barrack rooms we will have to live in, and already, I can foresee where our main suffering will come from. We will suffer more because of one another, being crowded and without privacy, than from our guards, whom we rarely see or will see. Here, German authority seems to be represented by a vociferous warrant officer who walks about the courtyard yelling all the time with his sword dangling in its sheath. He is typical of those barking officers who constitute the major strength of all the armies in the world. All we have to do is ignore him, but it is impossible to ignore thirty or thirty-five men whom chance has assigned to us as roommates. Of course everyone finds some cellmates friendly, some indifferent, some disagreeable, and some unbearable. Some people – and they are quite naive or quite optimistic – imagine that, because we are prisoners together, we all love one another like brothers. The former prisoners who suggest this are forgetting part of the truth: inaction and being thrown together are conducive to bringing out the worst in everyone. In the situation, judging already from each man's attitude and words, I can guess who will be unassuming, refined, generous, selfish, coarse, boastful, brutish, or a drunk. I came back from captivity fiercely opposed to and bitterly ironic about all social systems, past, present or future, which involve any amount of community living that doesn't allow the possibility for individuals to retire, at least at night, to some place which is his own, sheltered from other human beings. I believe that I must be considered in general as an aloof person.

When will we leave from here for a camp in Germany, a camp which we imagine as a paradise in comparison with this one, a paradise where we will be able to get out of our clothes and wash, where there will be beds and sheets, at least we think so? They tell us every day that it will be today, or tomorrow. 'They' means the ordinary soldiers and the vague non commissioned officers, who are the only Germans we see. Some of us knew this already: in the German army, officers are rare, don't mingle unnecessarily with underlings, don't interfere with their duties, and only appear on the scene to supervise. I don't think they are purposely deceiving us about the moment of our departure. The truth is that these subordinates don't know anything and only spread rumors, as is done in every military group everywhere. Who and where is the person with the authority to make decisions and to take charge of waiting for other prisoners or forming a convoy with those present? We have no idea. We will know we are leaving only one hour before departure. Some of us, who have for two years received and obeyed a hundred times marching orders for an unknown destination with only fifteen minutes preparation, are irritated by this lack of consideration.

Immediately on arrival, we are allowed to write one postcard each to our families and are told that this first communication is exempt from the automatic ten-day delay required of all prisoners' correspondence. The true fact is that this card took as long to reach its destination as later ones. Mine, written on June 2, did not arrive until June 28, two days after the first postcard sent from Mainz five days later. Were they lying to us? Right off, it seems undeniable. If it had left less than ten days late, it should have arrived approximately ten days earlier than the rest. It appears that someone was lying somewhere, but who and to whom? What became of the postcards sent from Stenay? They were clearly sent to Germany to then get to the Swiss border. Were they censored before their departure or kept along the way by some central bureau, which either didn't know about the promise or deliberately ignored it? Was it the order from the rear to lie to us at the front, and did the people who told the lie believe it? All this is not very clear to me, for, if indeed they were deliberately lying, that was a tactical error detrimental to the effect Germany would have preferred. It was to their advantage to give the impression that prisoners were being treated humanely and with consideration, to have them write home expressing satisfaction, thus indirectly undermining the morale of the enemy troops and population. Such a glaring deception would have been instantly spotted by any information bureau in Switzerland by simply comparing the dates and the so-called favor mentioned in many of these cards. It would surely inspire many of the deceived prisoners to make their anger known. It was a sure way to encourage the enemy to denounce one of Germany's 'lies.' You may say that Germany made many other psychological errors. Still this one was too gratuitous. After all, the most efficient means of undermining the morale of the adversary in this case, was not to pretend to treat prisoners well but to treat them well indeed, if one wanted to attract other Frenchmen to come and join them. The exemption of the delay for prisoners' first postcards was a cheap and effortless procedure, but they didn't apply it. I wonder if this doesn't show, after all, that not everything was perfect in the German organization or that somewhere the head of some post office found it easier not to perturb the order of his expeditions by giving priority to certain mail bags.

From the windows of our prison, we sadly look out onto the road we have come down as it ascends toward the front, Verdun and France. We can't see the town. Below us, there are some secondary military buildings, sheds, stables, and latrines. They show traces of a French air attack that happened a few days ago. I hear some say that they wish the French airplanes would come back and demolish it all. I wouldn't especially enjoy being destroyed in that way. A few

Russian prisoners pass by in their pale brown overcoats, with shovels on fatigue-duty, led by a German soldier. Poor humble friends, our hearts break for you. Your plight is so much worse than ours will ever be. No cards for you, no food packages, no beds, no sheets, nothing but the disgusting and insufficient daily grub, straw full of vermin to sleep on, the dirty, exhausting labor watched over by a guard who inevitably turns into a slave-driver. And do you even know what's going on, why you are here, what your chances are of making it? At least we can buy the *Ardenne Gazette*, a German paper written in French, and some other German papers. Of course they present only one side, but all other newspapers do the same. When confronted with a newspaper these days – in fact, at any time – it's not enough to read. One must interpret and each one interprets according to his strength and his temperament. The papers give all the official statements. I have rarely suspected systematic falsehoods in them. In the barracks everybody comments on these papers. What's important is that the French line has been re-established behind us after the assault that ran us down. Our being overrun has not been fatal for Verdun. Some officers, already believing their capture to be an important event, are writing down explanatory notes. Some, for lack of anything else to do, or perhaps wisely, play games with cards found in their pockets or at the canteen. In captivity as well as at the front, poker is the great favorite. Money is represented by pieces of paper with numbers written on them. One can imagine that, with this system, the stakes are high. Prisoners' poker will not always be as harmless. A kind philosopher from the left bank of the Meuse River (whom amazingly one of us has recognized as his best friend who happened to have been waiting for him here for two or three days) is peacefully reading the work of a deep thinker he always has in his pocket. We are all edgy, irritated, feverish, and short-tempered. Come on! Let them take us elsewhere, anywhere! Anything will be better than this stagnation!

The end comes on June 6 in the morning, when we are told we are leaving. We are ready in two minutes. I have regained some strength; to move is no longer a torture, only a pain. We are no longer as utterly destitute as we were a few days ago. The canteen sold us white cloth knapsacks, some toiletries and some mediocre food items. The prisoners' baggage, which will become quite substantial for the well-off among us, is beginning to accumulate, but for the moment we can easily carry it. They count and double count us, interspersing guards, who purposely show off loading their weapons in front of us. Let's go! We are afraid we will have to go through the town in full view of the local population. The ultimate shame is not to parade past the enemy's eyes but rather to file past our compatriots. The Germans could humiliate us this way, by swinging through the French town, an excellent way to depress the morale of occupied regions. The captors decide not to do so. The road from the barracks to the train station skirts the town, and we only come across a few Frenchmen. We stiffen, unable to speak, tears coming to our eyes. A road worker, old and bent, looks up from his toil, his face showing consternation when he sees us followed by a column of soldiers. The old man exclaims: 'Good God! Is it always going to be the same thing?' Walking by him, I say the classic phrase: 'We'll get 'em yet!' I believe that's all he hears from us as an answer. Yes, at that moment, I violently want us to get them. What are they doing here on this land that is not theirs? The presence of foreign uniforms in one's own country and the noise of weapons mixed with the sound of foreign voices are the most blatant forms of evil that the simplest of souls can understand and react to. It is the first evil that must be destroyed. Let the English stay in England, said Joan of Arc. I would add, let the Germans stay in Germany and the French in France. At least, let's not go into the neighboring country with swords and guns. We get to the train station, having, fortunately, seen only a few local inhabitants. Stupefied and pitiful, they say nothing and barely dare to look at us, seemingly terrified by the sight. We officers are quickly loaded into a third-class German train car while the enlisted men are locked into cattle cars that constitute the rest of the train. We are on our way to Germany.

The train is slow, the wheels are jolting us, and all my bones ache. At this speed, it will take at least twenty-four hours to reach Mainz, which, we were told, is our destination. I am remembering another trip, less than two years ago in a train that was taking us from the sunny South to the bleak province of Lorraine. It took us almost two days. As the commanding officer in charge of the police, I got off the train at each station to make sure things were orderly. We were in a first-class car, our uniforms were blue and red, which we thought, naively, was very practical on the field.[14] Songs echoed along the convoy and the train doors were decorated with flowers and flags. One eccentric fellow enjoying the cool air on the roof of the car got himself killed when the train passed through a tunnel, our first casualty. A reserve regiment, we were actually a bunch of civilians disguised as soldiers. I am dozing off. My comrades are not those of that trip; we all have helmets on and overcoats, which are sky blue underneath the persistent mud crust that we haven't been able to get rid of. And in a corner of the compartment sits a German infantryman in short boots and a round cap. The train has stopped for a moment in the open country. Instead of songs there is only deathly silence.

In the middle of the night they have us get off at a train station and wait a long time on the platform. We are at Kaiserslautern.[15] We are separated from the enlisted men, who continue toward an unknown destination. We get onto a regular train for Mainz, but first we are allowed to go, in small groups and carefully watched, to the station snack bar, where people barely look at us. Although it is our first and only stop here, other people like us have been passing through every day and night for months. Already they only sell artificial products that have replaced natural ones, 'ersatz' items limited in quantity for each customer. We are not treated any differently from other people. The waiters just politely refuse to sell us more than the regular ration. Certainly we are already far from the relative abundance of the canteens at the front, and these are hard times for Germany. Everything that is still edible is sent to the front and also to the metallurgical plants, which are making cannons and ammunition, like the steelworks of Lorraine we just saw blazing away near Hagondange.[16] Too bad we didn't load up on food supplies at Stenay, to the extent possible, even though the available items were nasty. Hunger, which will rarely leave me for several months, is starting to hurt. With an empty stomach and feeling a little light-headed, I get into the train car under the indifferent eyes of a few civilians. In a state of half-torpor, I watch as we pass the banks of the Rhine. From the train window, I can see pretty little houses, the carefully cultivated countryside, the Worms cathedral, and a camp for Russian prisoners in Worms with cannons at each corner aimed at the center. And still in this state, I get off the train with my companions at the station in south Mainz, outside the city proper, and after a five-minute walk up a steep path, arrive at the Citadel, towering ominously above the railroad. A heavy double door opens to let us in. I catch a glimpse of a courtyard with a few trees, where French, Belgian, English, and Russian officers are exercising in uniforms that seem splendid in comparison with our downtrodden garb. The door closes behind us. Today is June 17, 1916, and I will not leave this place until eighteen months later, on December 7, 1917.

Notes

1. La Caillette refers to a wooded ravine about four miles north-east of the Fort of Verdun. Georges Connes received the Verdun Medal with a citation letter indicating he had fought at Chauvoncourt, Bois Chevalier, Les Eparges, Etang de Vaux and La Caillette, all local villages or sites where battles were fought. Close by are other sites well-known for having been bombarded relentlessly, captured and recaptured many times: Vaux Fort, Douaumont, Mort Homme, Hill 304. The Battle of Verdun refers to all battles that were fought in the area over a period of almost two years (February 1916 to August 1917).

Most of the last names of fellow combatants had originally been indicated by initials in the manuscript. Later on, probably at the time Connes wrote final notations, some were completed. These additions are indicated in brackets.

2. The Douaumont Fort, located about one and a half miles from La Caillette, was in German hands by then.

3. The village of Souville is about one mile south of La Caillette.

4. Connes appears to have spent only five or ten minutes in Douaumont, which seemed to him to be a safe, if temporary shelter. He did not notice the traces of the explosion that three weeks earlier had killed 679 Germans.

5. This is an allusion to the battle of Jutland (May 31, 1916). The enormous battle took place off the coast of Denmark between the German High Seas Fleet and the British Grand Fleet. Although the losses for the British (6,274) were much heavier than those of the Germans (2,545), the broad effects of the battle left the British fleet the undisputed master of the high seas.

6. Neuilly is a suburb west of Paris.

7. Azanne is a village located about three miles north of Douaumont.

8. Georges Demartial is the author of *Comment on mobilisa les consciences* (How we were brainwashed). Demartial, whom one could describe as a pacifist polemist, had gone as far as to demonstrate that France and her allies were, in the final analysis, responsible for the war. In 1927–28, he was prosecuted for his position. As Sirinelli recounts (*Les Intellectuels en France de L'Affaire Dreyfus à nos Jour*, p. 444–53) his name was removed from the Legion of Honor. This affair is a good illustration of the hostile climate of the 1920s when Connes was trying to publish his memoir. During the Second World War, Demartial again brought forth his belief that France bore the responsibility for starting the war and consequently was considered by the Collaboration press as a 'good worker for Franco-German reconciliation.' The direction taken by Connes, this other pacifist, was exactly the opposite.

9. Turpinite, a new explosive, was invented by Eugène Turpin. The 'steamroller' is a metaphor representing the hopes that the powerful Russian force was going to smash the German line.

10. Stenay is a small town north-west of Azanne.

11. Connes seems to have visited Germany only once before. In August 1908 he had witnessed the national mourning for the catastrophe of the zeppelin L 74 near Stuttgart.

12. An *uhlan* was a cavalryman bearing a lance in German, Austrian and Polish armies. This vision of Connes evokes the somewhat quixotic caricatures by such artists as Daumier and Hansi that were seen during the Franco-Prussian War (1870–71). The 1914 battle of the Marne River was one of the bloodiest stages of the war and a temporary victory for the Allied Forces.

13. Bélisaire is a recurring character in Alphonse Daudet's short stories. This average Frenchman specializes in ambushing Germans (commonly called Prussians at the time because Prussia was the dominant German province).

14. In 1914 the French were attired in long dark blue tunics (black for officers) with red pants and white gloves. In late 1914 light blue uniforms were adopted.

15. Kaiserslautern is a city in Germany located about thirty miles from the French border.

16. Hagondange, a city in France, is about twenty-five miles from Verdun.

2

Mainz: Prison Induction, the 'Salting Tub'

We naively imagine that as soon as we enter the Citadel, we will be treated like everyone else and will be free to mingle with the comrades we have just seen. We are quickly disabused. They hurry us, pushing us about as if we had the plague. Our future companions, obviously aware of what's in store for us, are content to observe from a distance, pausing a moment in their walk but making no attempt to communicate with us, apart from a few motions of the hand and a few words of welcome. Barely half a minute and thirty yards later, a new door closes behind us, separating us from the outside world. Because there are so many of us, we will be here for several days in the hermetically sealed space, which one of the earlier prisoners (nobody remembers who) had baptized the 'salting tub.' The name was faithfully passed on and preserved; it was difficult to find a more fitting one.

The purpose of the 'salting tub,' according to most of those who were put in it, was to 'cure.' It seemed to me at the time to be an unnecessary cruelty or even a refinement of underhanded craftiness. I needed time and reflection to realize that such a procedure, whatever its way of functioning, was essential in a camp for officer-prisoners and perfectly relevant to the logic of the situation.[1] I don't know whether in France they were naive enough to let the new arrivals mingle with the earlier 'boarders' right away. If they did, they were very foolish. I believe that in prisons all over the world any incoming 'guest' is first submitted to a search in order to rid him of anything that might be contrary to the rules of the place and help him escape. Our being put in solitary confinement is the equivalent of this search. Whether the procedure is legitimate or not, I don't think that any reasonable person could have serious doubts. From the first day, could one leave weapons, maps, compasses, and money in the prisoners' possession? It would be ridiculous, like setting

29

yourself up for punishment. However, what irritated us so much, most of my comrades and myself, was probably less the system itself than the way it was applied and what we considered their insincerity and deceit. At the risk of offending many excellent comrades, I have no qualms about stating that this process seems to me to have solved the problem with a certain elegance.

The goal of our captors is to draw up a complete inventory of what the officers own, while avoiding the disgrace of disputes and the unpleasant experience and uncertainties of a body search, which common-law criminals are subjected to. I don't know whether or not international conventions prohibited such searches of prisoners. There are no two ways to go about it: the prisoners must strip to their bare skin, thus shedding their clothes and everything they possess. The pretext for this operation is a shower for us and the disinfecting of our clothes, an explanation that seems to be reasonable. There is no doubt that we very much need a wash. A nation that is more hygiene-conscious than the French can rightly assert that everything connected with the army sorely needs to be sterilized. As a matter of fact, I don't think anyone refused the refreshing shower and the temporary separation from his clothing. Was it possible to refuse? And what would happen if someone refused? Confinement to the cell? Being undressed and put in the shower by force? I have no idea. I don't even know if it ever occurred. So far, nothing had happened that was not sufficiently justifiable, but then came the 'bag trick,' a performance as classical as that of the 'salting tub.'

Here is how the operation goes: we are locked up in groups of seven or eight – field officers in smaller groups – in rooms that all open onto the same hallway patrolled by a sentry. Each room has only one window, which opens onto the courtyard, but the window-panes are frosted with white paint and the windows nailed shut. Moreover, we have been warned that the police station, situated just below us, has orders to shoot if they perceive any attempt to communicate with the outside world. They also have orders, as we will learn later, to prevent anyone from approaching prisoners when they are walking outside 'free,' if one can call it that. We are truly in solitary confinement. By scratching on the frosted glass, we can just about see some branches moving slightly in the breeze and, beyond, the outline of a building. They bring each of us a shirt, shorts, and a pair of socks, informing us that these items will be deducted from our pay. They tell us to lay all our clothes on our beds with our name on a label. In a cloth bag hanging at the foot of the bed we must put the total contents of our pockets. Then, draped in blankets, carrying the new underwear and a piece of soap, which will be taken out of our pay too, we are led to the basement shower room. They have achieved their goal; you could even say they have played their trick: we are now separated from everything we arrived with, and the administration can easily enter the room we have just left, take our clothes to the sterilizing room and the bags with our treasures to the main office. They can then search the beds and the lockers, where some clever fellows have tried to hide their most precious possessions. For those who have something they want to conceal, all they have left is the secret recesses of their bodies, and some make use of that. Unfortunately, these natural orifices cannot shelter anything very large.

We look like a carnival procession, a student parade,[2] or a Roman march, whatever you like, as we head for a wonderful shower, which barely begins to remove the dirt and dust that have accumulated during these past days. All this takes place under the stern, scrutinizing eyes of a warrant officer, who doesn't say a word. I see a scale and weigh myself. I'm terrified! At six feet I normally weigh 168 pounds; now I am down to 145. We go back to our room and, of course, during this excursion and until we leave the 'salting tub' we will never meet any comrades from the neighboring rooms. The system requires it. When we want to go to the bathroom, we knock on the door and an orderly accompanies us, never more than one at a time, to an enclosed place at the end of the hallway. No door ever opens unless the others are closed and all occupants are inside.

When we come back 'home,' naively, we are surprised and annoyed to see that not only our clothes (we were prepared for that) but also the famous bags containing our personal possessions have disappeared. They did promise, didn't they, that we would find them, untouched, at the very place we had left them? Everyone's memory is different. One person says one thing, someone else another. I believe we hadn't paid much attention to what they said. I believe we were told that we would get them back with their contents, but without our captors saying where or when. In fact, we will get them back with their contents a little later. I think we had actually convinced ourselves that we had been promised the bags would never leave the foot of our beds. Thinking about it now, I wonder if we weren't unrealistic when we imagined that the German guards would give us out of kindness the ideal means to hide exactly what we wanted from searches aimed precisely at discovering such items.

It's amusing to think that it wasn't necessarily those who had tried to hide something in the bags who were the most indignant! They just didn't trust this bag procedure and were now furious to have been tricked. Certainly, for many of the 'guests' of the 'salting tub,' the 'bag trick' remains a symbol of 'German treachery.'

Why this shameful subterfuge, you might ask, and why not simply ask the prisoners to empty their pockets? That would have meant demanding trust from the jailers and not from the prisoners: this was war. Half or even three-quarters of the prisoners, had they been asked to do this, would have hidden everything they could, would have felt no remorse about doing so, and would even have gloated about it. The duty of the officer-prisoner is to escape, and all means to this end are honorable, right? Remember that we were forbidden to give our word of honor, except later, concerning taking walks. Nine-tenths of us thought we had no duty to be honest with the enemy, but that didn't prevent us from vigorously reproaching the enemy for their lack of honesty. As is well known, practices harmful to the enemy are praiseworthy when we apply them but reprehensible when the enemy uses them against us.

It's only on the third day of our 'being cured,' toward evening on June 10, that they begin to take us one by one from our rooms, after bringing back our clothes, which show traces of having been disinfected and searched. No lining has been left unexplored nor the soles of our shoes, especially the heels. We are called out one by one and, of course, whoever goes out never comes back to tell us of his impressions. He goes to the outside world, the normal world of prisoners. But now we know roughly what is in store for us. In order to become official prisoners, we must be interrogated, after witnessing the opening and inventory of our treasure bags. We learnt this from the Belgian soldier after we returned from the showers and found our possessions gone. The Belgian started playing the role of orderly for us by making our purchases at the canteen. For many of us, the Belgian soldier seemed suspicious. I personally never had any reason to think he was anything other than a clever guy who, having found a cushy job, wanted to keep it. He was allowed to come to us only after he could no longer be of use to us by warning us about the search, for instance, or accepting to hide something for us. And, besides, what could he have done against us? Report on things we said? Are the things we say worth reporting and worth anyone's attention?

We spent those days, still dressed up as Romans, eating, sleeping, talking, and playing cards. Poker started again, this time with match

32

sticks serving as money. I learned later that more gambling had started in adjacent rooms.

There is no doubt that the meals we were served there were the best we received during our captivity, and infinitely better than what we would eat in the common prison. I don't think I am exaggerating when I say the proportion was like three to one. There was an abundance of a thick soup, very edible potatoes, spinach, and every day at noon, a measurable slice of meat. Was it a trap to entice us to write home that we were sufficiently fed? If it was a trap, I fell into it. My letter from Mainz only requested money, some sweets, and warm underwear. The last night in Douaumont I had taken off my sweater in order to do some digging. It had remained buried there, and during this very cold beginning of June, weakened and underfed, I was freezing. Because of this mistake of not asking for more provisions from home, I half-starved for three months. It took this long for me to realize that we prisoners could not be fed by our captors. I had to make my family understand that it was up to them to feed me. Finally, a succession of packages started arriving, which allowed me to eat enough to halfway satisfy my appetite, then later to fully take care of my hunger. In this case again, was there a systematic deceit? If there was, I can't quite understand it. I don't really know what to believe. What result was achieved by this? For a few days, they raised our hopes, and consequently those of our families, about how prisoners were fed and therefore about food supplies in Germany. But once these days were over, there began for us a reaction proportionate to our surprise and our disappointment, and our letters were full of requests for biscuits and canned food. After describing ourselves as satisfied, we were starting to cry hunger. Wasn't that giving us the means of confirming the fact that German shortages were increasing? And didn't all the observers stationed in Switzerland see the influx of food packages going to the prisoners? Could one say that the Germans acted this way purely to make us suffer a few more days? That would seem to me almost understandable – it was war, wasn't it? To make the enemy tighten their belts for a few more days when they were soon going to enjoy an abundance of food in front of their starving guards cannot seem like a terrible crime in the eyes of super-patriots. I ended up wondering whether, given the rather weak appetite of individuals who are locked up twenty-four hours a day, we didn't end up exaggerating, in retrospect, the quantity and the quality of meals served in the 'salting tub.'

Concerning our mail, we are informed that each month we are allowed to send two six-page letters and four postcards that conform to the official format. We will find writing paper and cards at the canteen. Our correspondence must be written in pencil; it will then be kept for ten days before being sent on and, of course, will be censored. All attempts to convey to the enemy any military or economic information would cause us to be court-martialed. Any unfounded complaints about the functioning of the camp would bring about disciplinary measures. We can receive letters, postcards, and books in unlimited numbers but no newspaper or any written material concerning the war. In any case, censorship takes care of sorting out what can and cannot be received. We can also ask our families to send us clothes and as much solid or liquid food as we want, after they pass inspection, of course. In my own case, and as far as I could tell, these rules were always faithfully followed. Only once, in 1917, because of some sort of dispute about the system, the packages were retained for a few days but the accumulated goods were returned to us. This information is given to us directly by the officer in charge of censorship, a lieutenant Schmitt or Schmied, whom I personally find disagreeable as a censor, not as a person. His duty is to prevent and discover our tricks and cheating. He is a censor; he censors. An ugly job, isn't it? However, it is well known that the person who practices it for our benefit against our prisoners is . . . OK, while he who practices it against us for the benefit of the enemy is . . . etc. So all of us agree: Mr. Schmitt is a disgusting individual.[3]

On the evening of June 10, I still have not been called out. Only two or three of us are left, and our interrogations are postponed until tomorrow. That's my luck! The next day they are probably busy with other rooms, they are not in a hurry, and it's already late in the day when they come for me at last. The orderly takes me to the office. I am expecting to face important individuals and diplomats crafty as foxes. How mistaken I am! There is only one private there, a man with glasses and a goatee who doesn't even speak French well. I thought I was being brought before some under-machiavel and all I see is a pen-pusher, not at all happy about the thankless job that has been dumped on him. The conversation drags along. He does not believe in what he is doing. My regiment? My company? I can easily tell him the numbers, which I have already written on a form we had to fill out. How many men? Who was on the right? On the left? I forgot this or I don't know. How is the French morale? Fine, of course! Do the French believe the war will last long? Uh . . . two, three years. We don't converse any further. He knows as well as I do, along with everyone else here and everywhere, that this cross-examination of an officer-prisoner is nothing but a ridiculous formality leading nowhere and is still performed only because it is customary. In this case, it is almost ludicrous. The interrogator's mastery of the subtleties of the French language is very poor, and some of the individuals questioned make fun of him with impunity. Lieutenant Schmitt's French was better, and he was much more clever. When he himself led the interrogation, the conversation, it seemed, had another tone. The fact that he usually put a subordinate in charge of this nasty job shows how few illusions he had about the usefulness of this procedure.

When entering the office, I find on the table the bag that contains everything I had in my pockets four days ago, that is to say almost nothing in my case. A warrant officer opens it in my presence. There is no reason to think that he might have opened it before now. What it contains cannot get lost; he is sure to find it when he opens the packet. He sorts the contents into three piles, as the case may be. First: war spoils; the second: objects belonging to the prisoner but which he is not allowed to keep because the items could facilitate an escape (the list is long and sometimes surprising); and third: objects belonging to the prisoner that he can keep. The objects in the second category are confiscated but will be returned to the owner at the end of his captivity. These items follow him if he is transferred to another camp. I imagine the practice could not exactly correspond to the theory. The German administration had serious worries in 1917 and 1918, and a lot of things no doubt got lost in November and December 1918. I also imagine that the owners probably didn't waste a lot of time looking for their possessions and claiming them.

They didn't give me back my blanket, which since Douaumont was my only possession, along with my clothes, helmet and shoes. Apparently blankets are war spoils. As a matter of fact, I had not paid for it from my own pocket; it belonged to the French army.

It's over. I am told I am assigned to room 40 of Building II. I am sent through a door, shown a corridor and a staircase, which I follow, soon finding myself dazed by the sunlight, stunned by the open space, a little lightheaded, slightly unsteady on my legs, and 'free' in a space of about ninety by ninety yards along with some 500 other prisoners.

Notes

1. This effort of reflection is Connes's central theme. If he had known Romain Rolland's *Au-dessus de la Mêlée*, he could have taken as his motto the following phrase: 'I need to understand my opponent's reasons. I do not like to believe in bad faith. I believe he is as passionate and sincere as I am. Why wouldn't we make an effort to understand each other' (p. 84).

2. The reference here is to the 'Ball of the Four Arts,' an annual party given by the Fine Arts School where attendees wore picturesque costumes, one of which was going naked.

3. Sandre, also captured at Douaumont, had gone through Mainz and the 'salting tub' three months earlier. He also had to deal with the censor Schmidt, whom Sandre, in *Le Purgatoire*, describes as 'smooth-tongued, smirking, officious and giving the impression of being cruel and false' (p. 84). Further on, Sandre describes another censor as being 'certainly the most cruel, underhanded and relentless officer in the whole bunch . . . He resembled Mainz's Herr Schmidt like a brother' (p. 158).

3

The Citadel at Mainz: Eighteen Months

The Citadel at Mainz probably has its origins as a Roman camp that served as a bulwark of Latin civilization on the Rhine. Built on a small hill, well situated and high enough to allow a view of the confluence of the Rhine and Main rivers, it probably was used by the Roman legion to observe the barbarians and keep them on the other side of the Rhine. Called Drusus's Tower or Drusus's Tomb, a structure remains, the origin and purpose of which are not known, which appears to be Roman indeed for it is the base of a tower, built in drystone and still standing about thirty-six feet high and twelve or fifteen feet in diameter. Goethe came to see it and, he says, to draw it.[1] Today, one can see at its foot, surrounded by chicken wire, the brick building where our pitiful food was prepared and eaten. Several of the French prisoners also knew, so everybody soon found out, that the French had been besieged at Mainz in 1793 and had been garrisoned specifically in this citadel, which passed back and forth between the French and the enemy until the end of the German Empire. These memories excited some of the thinkers among us who felt they were the descendants of Latin culture which would return and occupy Mainz, as they announced to the barbarians with whom they had a chance to talk.[2] I myself didn't believe any of it. In 1919, I went back to visit Mainz as a free man. In the Citadel I found Latin culture represented by a Senegalese battalion.

My visit to Mainz in 1919 was prompted by curiosity: I wanted to see something of this city where I had spent a year and a half, longer than I ever spent in any city except for some in France, and of which I had seen almost nothing except for a suburban train station with its commuters coming and going. Also visible from the windows of the front building, were some children playing or, in winter, sliding down the path that led up to our entrance, the top stories of a few houses beyond the trench where the railroad plunged almost directly under the Citadel into a tunnel toward the Central Station. We could see the tower and the small spires of the cathedral, red or rather ochre colored, that we drew a hundred times, with more or less success, having plenty of leisure time on our hands. In the distance we could see the Rhine with its passing steamboats (too far for us to distinguish any interesting details), an immense metal bridge spanning the railroad toward the south, and the junction of the Main with the Rhine. Beyond the bridge there was a hilly countryside; toward the north, the heights of the Taunus Mountains with Wiesbaden looking like a white blotch below it.[3] That is all we could see of Mainz. The picture when painted or described may seem very rich. In fact, it is very pretty; we would have much worse views to look at, and we would never tire of contemplating it. Comparing it with other camps where we saw only four walls, it was picturesque and charming, but one cannot be content with landscapes for very long. A person's main interest is in other human beings. We often wondered what there was to see on the other side of the walls that limited our view from the other buildings located behind the ramparts. We would have given a lot to see it. In 1919 I saw beyond the walls: there is nothing there, except totally ordinary things, a boulevard, streets, houses . . .

The Citadel is truly a Vauban-type structure with an earth platform totally surrounded and supported by walls 30–45 feet high on the side of the city, lower on the opposite side.[4] We are perched on this terreplein and completely encircled by wire fencing and metal grating. Around this grating there is a first line of sentries. Encircling the foot of the ramparts, a second cordon stands guard. If someone wanted to escape, it would be necessary to break through both. We are housed in three buildings: the first, which I just called the front one, on the city side, is the only one directly built on the surrounding wall, straddling the main entrance. When we look out from its front windows, all that separates us from the street and freedom is iron bars, a twenty-five- or forty-five-foot leap, depending on which floor you are on, and the sentries. Plus, at night, there is glaring electrical lighting. The second building (by the way, called Building III) forms a right angle with the first one. It contains the police station, the 'salting tub' and the canteen. Also, on the ground floor, there are some prison cells with vaulted ceilings and barred windows looking toward the back. These two massively-built structures appear to date from the early nineteenth century. Finally, the last structure, Building II, entirely separate from the first two and parallel to the front one, is brand new. It had just been built in 1914 and was supposed to be a cadet school, but now prisoners are its first occupants. Its washrooms and toilets are well arranged. The latter, with standard-type lavatory seats, have no doors. We are like horses, each in his stall, and one has to do one's business in public. Why this precaution of having no doors? I will leave the explanation to psychologists. By the way, this detail of barrack accommodations is one we will protest against, eventually winning our cause and obtaining doors. Apparently, international conventions require that officer-prisoners have doors. In the other, older buildings, there is no lack of toilet facilities either. On the fourth side, a separate block houses the *Kommandantur* (local military command post) and the offices; a hangar is divided into a library and a reading room, a canteen, and a theater. At the foot of the Roman tower, as I have mentioned, between Buildings II and III, are the kitchen and dining rooms.

I need to emphasize that it's only during the day that we are free to circulate between these buildings inside the surrounding walls. From nightfall until morning, we are locked up in our various buildings and sentries take over the corridors, one on each floor. Their heavy boots and weapons resound all night just outside our doors. Later, we will request (and our request will be granted) that their boots be replaced by slippers. Any prisoners found outside after nightfall would be shot without warning. Of course, everything is floodlit. The time for opening and closing depends on the season. In winter we are locked up from 4:30 p.m. to 7:30 a.m., fifteen hours out of twenty-four, which amounts to almost half the time over the whole year. We are trapped indeed, and the Prussian organization keeps us well in its claws. During these eighteen months, although scores of individuals are brainstorming the idea of escape, no one, absolutely no one, succeeds in escaping from the Citadel.

I will only become aware of all these facts later. For the moment I just need to find my place in the room I have been assigned to. It is occupied solely by new prisoners like me, who just arrived a few hours ago. I can't expect to learn anything from them except their impressions of the 'salting tub.' We are not destined to stay together for long. Chance has thrown use together here to begin with, but I already know that this is not a permanent arrangement. The first necessity for a prisoner is to integrate himself into a group whose members, to the extent possible, he finds congenial. This is hard. To my knowledge, the camp administration has never refused requests for changes when they are reasonable and practical, but weeks and months often went by before a vacancy occurred in the coveted room. It was necessary to plot, maneuver, use tricks and be on the watch for departures. Very often a room was divided between two groups, or even more, some of which were in favor of and others against the new candidate. Admitting a newcomer is not unimportant. You have to put up with all his peculiarities and his faults. We are living in very close quarters here. For months, years, a single room serves as bedroom, bathroom, dining room, study and work room for three, seven, ten or twelve junior officers, according to the room's size. The beds are most often double bunks as in the cabin of a transatlantic liner. It is a question of choosing companions whose peculiarities and faults coincide with yours. There are some awkward characters whom no one wants and who wander about, tossed from one room to another, a week here, two weeks there, never satisfied and never acceptable to anyone. Most of the time, though, solid groups finally form that last for years, except when men leave or change to another camp, only disbanding at the end of the prison term. No one will be astonished to hear me say that even within congenial groups, the reality of continuously living together, crowded in this way inevitably brings about quarrels. Constant contact with one's neighbors ended up rubbing people the wrong way. The most peaceful individuals got angry about nothing, little things, anything and everything. Then one day things blew up violently, but usually not for long. In every room offensive words were exchanged. In almost every room, at some time or other, it was necessary to separate two combatants. One always helps in such cases because one might need to be helped in turn.

Leaving my room-mates I go outside for the first time, where I join the pitiful procession that walks incessantly around the courtyard, one by one, two by two, or in bunches of three or four, always turning in the same direction, counter-clockwise, the positive direction as a mathematician would say. Who decided that we would go around this way, from right to left, rather than from left to right? Only a few rare nonconformists walk in the opposite direction. Are they rebelling against custom? I thought that, as a newcomer, I would attract attention, but no one pays any attention to me. The comrades from my detachment who came from the 'salting tub' before me have probably satisfied people's curiosity. Several days will pass before I make anyone's acquaintance or meet individuals whom I knew directly or indirectly, or classmates. And then, by an extraordinary chance, out of the 'salting tub' will come a small group of friends who were with me at the beginning of the campaign, whose destiny I will share from then on. For the moment, I can observe without being observed. The general impression of the splendor of these prisoners that I had received on first arriving and quickly crossing the courtyard now fades on closer examination. The British officers from the regular force captured near Mons and Charleroi seem to come directly from their Piccadilly Square tailors and seem not to notice anybody.[5] They would walk right over you without blinking. Throughout the hallways, always impeccable, they pass by you or prepare their meals on the stoves without looking at anyone. It's by seeing them that one understands the difference between the verbs *ignorer* in French (simply not to know) and *to ignore* in English (to voluntarily pay no attention to someone or something). They will all leave in about ten days, to no one's regret I believe. Their opulence is an insult to our pitiful state. From then on, we will rarely see any Brits, only a few aviators or colonial troops now and then who are much closer to ordinary human beings. The Russians, all well clothed and groomed, come a close second to the British for correctness, but with as much nonchalance as the others have arrogance. The French and the Belgians are clearly wearing out their old peacetime uniforms. It's impossible not to feel that there are several types of men present here who cohabit but don't mingle. It's only the official language of 1916 that claimed that the prisoners from the Allied nations formed one unit against the Germans and that attempts to divide them only brought them closer together. The Germans were too clever not to benefit from this opportunity to make their enemies, as they were temporarily gathered, aware of all that set us apart from one another. The fact that, through a quirk of European politics, one finds oneself on the same side for a while does not create natural affinities. The French patriotic press, in 1925, hardly talks about France's fraternity with Russia and England anymore. On this June 11, 1916, I am aware of these deep differences.

All the British are wearing on their left sleeve a black armband for the loss of Kitchener.[6] Building I is flying the flag of the German Empire with a black eagle on a white background. When I ask why I am told it is to celebrate the capitulation of Fort Vaux a few days ago. Commanding Officer Raynal and his officers are in the 'salting tub.'

The day after my arrival, the newcomers are introduced to the colonel who is the camp commander. I find this a courteous procedure. It suggests we still exist as men and as officers. The ceremony

41

is simple and correct. They have us go through the gate that separates the courtyard and the *Kommandantur*, and stand in line next to others in front of the building. The colonel, a Prussian officer, rather small, perfectly correct, reviews our line-up. Rumor immediately has it that he is remnant of Sadowa. For the French, all the German camp commanders are leftovers from Sadowa.[7] He stops in front of each one of us, accompanied by a warrant officer who informs him of our names and ranks, and he salutes us. We salute him back. It seems like a scene from the glorious past. A little further, at right angles to us, they line up eight or ten British navy officers who were rescued in the Skagerrack Straits at the very moment we were being picked up in front of Douaumont. All ages and ranks are represented, from the gray-haired naval commander to the beardless and rosy-cheeked midshipmen. They present the appearance of people who have been shipwrecked indeed. One has neither boots nor shoes but only a type of sock that is worn inside wooden shoes. The 'remnant from Sadowa' approaches, stops in front of the first officer and salutes. The Brit looks at him without flinching. The interpreter officer tells him in English that he is supposed to salute the colonel, who then salutes him again. The British officer remains impassive and looks him straight in the eye, making no movement. The colonel salutes the second British officer with the same result, makes an about-face and, livid, returns to his office. Several of us, and some of the spectators behind the fence react in a curious way: the patriot in us approves the insult to the enemy; the soldier disapproves the offence to the man who, according to military conventions, is undeniably our chief. Pride of the English facing the foreigner; pride of the seaman facing the landlubber, this spectacle is a new one for these spectators. What is a Prussian colonel next to a lieutenant in His Majesty's Navy! As for me, in this scene I will never forget, I see the clash between two forms of evil, two inflexible castes, two brands of human pride, which must disappear if the world is ever to improve, and which will disappear, leaving room for others! One of the two is dead already or almost.

I am hungry. I can't deny it to myself anymore. Every night I wake up long before dawn in a sweat, my belly torn by the sensation of emptiness, and I try in vain to go back to sleep. Who made up the idiotic saying that 'he who sleeps doesn't need to eat'? Once maybe, but not every day. During the day, I wander around sadly, sometimes forced to stop, feeling lightheaded. Later I will be told that one could see daylight through me at that time. I was frightened to find myself weighing 145 pounds; soon it will be 143, then 138. Meanwhile, the people who have been prisoners longer than us, provided with comfortable provisions they have accumulated through the packages they have been receiving, are wondering what they will treat themselves to every night. I have found only one classmate among them, Tétaud,[8] an excellent fellow, who helps me by giving me some canned food. I gather other starving individuals, and we are each able to eat a few mouthfuls of good food, just enough to stimulate our hunger and make us realize even more sharply the insufficiency and mediocrity of what we are served at the canteen. It's ridiculous: three potatoes, not always edible, two spoonfuls of spinach or sorrel, which will soon stop being spinach or sorrel and become some sort of weed, a piece of meat the size of a nut, a tiny piece of cheese, and less than an ounce of white bread, which will soon disappear. Sometimes we are offered 'fish in aspic,' nothing but cartilage in gelatin. In the evening a nondescript gruel and a cup of some 'ersatz' cocoa. Every Monday we receive for the week a block of about three pounds of K bread. I will not even describe K bread.[9] The wise individuals immediately cut marks for the seven days of the week; the short-sighted have nothing left by Thursday or Friday. The canteen also sells some excellent cheese, but there is not as much as we want and not for everyone. We stand in line at the door until the canteen opens. I am one of these people who, if in a group waiting for a bus or standing waiting for a seat, are always the ones left out. Only once or twice will I succeed in getting some of that cheese. My salvation is the jars of jam – probably made without sugar or fruit – that are available. I eat almost one a day without any bread. The cheese will disappear for good as early as my first week in Mainz and the jam the second week. The Russian officers, who for the most part cannot receive any packages, are strictly limited to this diet. The German guards have very little to eat – our orderlies can easily see what the guards receive. The civilian population also has a limited food supply. But, of course, when one is free, one can manage to supplement these rations. I am hungry.

If, during those two and a half years, I had depended solely on the official rations distributed by the administration, I am convinced I never would have made it out of Germany alive.

The officer-prisoners have nothing to do to keep themselves busy. The conventions forbid making us work. It is our damnation. We would be delighted to dig up potatoes or move gravel, but these distractions are forbidden to us. What does one do to kill so much time? Some poor fellows, not in the habit of using their brains in order to fill in their leisure time, have never gotten the hang of it. There is one guy whose sole activity consists of announcing the time. He learns that it is 2:45 or 5:30 and believes he has to inform his companions about it, a good way to exasperate his fellow prisoners to the point where one explodes.

The prisoners have no other obligation than to answer the roll-call twice a day, at 9 a.m. and at 4, 5, or 6 p.m. according to the season. No wake-up call, no morning reveille. For the 9 a.m. call, the lazy ones get up at 8:55 or 8:57 and rush into the courtyard. In theory, to attend the roll-call, one must wear the regular correct uniform, but in practice, pants, an overcoat and a fatigue cap will do. We stand in line, grouped by rooms, in the order of our numbers, each group in front of its building, on three sides of a square. A German officer walks rapidly in front of us, his hand to his cap, saluting, accompanied by a warrant officer who carries the daily duty sheet. At a glance they know if everyone in each room is present. We return the salute and that's it. Occasionally, someone is late. The German officer stops in front of that group until the laggard arrives, cursed (inwardly) by all the others who are forced to stand there. The roll-call takes place whatever the weather, so we have no desire for it to drag on. One can always have oneself reported ill by a room-mate. The warrant officer writes down the name he receives, then goes to the room to check on those named before giving the signal to dismiss. This signal is given as soon as the roll-call is over, if there are no special announcements. If there is something to be communicated, the service officer signals to us to form a circle around him. The person who played this role at Mainz was Captain Von Tecklenburg, tall, correct, elegant, dressed in the long blue tunic of the old uniform and ordinarily escorted by a hound dog called Max. He spoke French quite well. Of course he made mistakes. How many among us wouldn't have made many more in German? With an off-handedness which, I admit, bordered on rudeness we laughed in his face. Surprised, he would stop speaking, not understanding what was going on. Von Tecklenburg was hated by almost all those who went through the Mainz camp and, in my opinion, very unfairly. They blamed him for a duplicity that they were determined to identify as a characteristic of German behavior. The French are all candid as children aren't they? Von Tecklenburg was no more deceitful than the average person. He was a Prussian officer of the old school. He had no love for us; the opposite would have been indeed very curious! The situation forced him to treat the mortal enemies of everything he revered with a respect which he must have felt to be very exaggerated. Just put yourself in his place: he tried to be clever and often didn't succeed. He was what his caste and his education had made him: a good monarchist, a good patriot, a good soldier, probably even a good Christian, all virtues that some of us would have found worthy of admiration, if only he had been French. No one can accuse him of ever having made an improper gesture or said a rude word. The defeat and demise of the old Germany must have broken his heart. The prisoners hated him. They even hated his dog, an innocent creature who often got kicked in the rear in a cowardly manner when no Germans were looking.

Von Tecklenburg was, more specifically, chief of Building II, the most important. Building III's destiny was presided over by a weird fellow, the strangest and the most amusing (a rare quality) of the German officers I had a chance to meet. I forget his name, Schroeder, maybe. He was part English and spoke English as easily as German. He was tall, lean, and a little bent forward when he walked. He was clean-shaven and his nose made him resemble the puppet Polichin- elle.[10] He had an unusual quality for a German officer: a sense of humor. His small eyes were always twinkling mischievously and he seemed to be constantly enjoying the humbug of the whole affair. He didn't hide his feelings. Neutral, no longer young, and free from any burden of illusions, he was contemplating the spectacle of the world with benevolent irony. How did this joker happen to be a captain in the German army, even as a reservist? I never could figure it out, and he himself must have been most astonished. He was the one we went to for tricky problems, because we were sure to deal with an intelligent man, free from prejudice. In 1917, when we put together a comic performance in the courtyard, authorized by the not-too-astute censorship, we presented him dressed in an overcoat and a top hat but perfectly recognizable and singing songs about his neutrality. Finally, Building I was under the direction of 'the porcelain maker.' He was another reserve captain who happened to own a china store in town. Colonel Raynal told me later that when he was garrisoned in Mainz in 1919, he met the 'porcelain man,' who bowed very low to him. This 'porcelain man' was more like a bull in a china shop. Dark haired, he would roll his eyes, his moustache would bristle up, and he would walk about in a great jingling of spurs and saber. Probably because of his civilian profession, he had been put in charge of the prestigious surveillance of kitchens and dining halls.

One day we were clicking our spoons against our glasses to protest the fact that our meager meal was late, and he quelled our concert by yelling at us – unworthy behavior on both sides, but we had started it. These three officers, along with the colonel, whom we rarely saw, and the censor, made up the permanent staff of the camp. A few lieutenants, some brutal and coarse, others gentle and refined, only passed through the camp on their way to the front.

Below these high personages crawls a small population of shirkers, non-commissioned officers and employees, the ones who really make things work. Why are they here? Except for one or two, none of them is visibly inadequate for more active and more dangerous service. Yet, I will never see any of them disappear, even when, as we did in France, Germany is scraping the bottom of the barrel in order to recruit anyone capable of bearing arms. I imagine that there, like everywhere else, the shifty ones remain the shifty ones. A Jew from Frankfurt who effectively does all the censorship work and presides over the distribution of packages – an important responsibility, as I will soon explain; a young man with an influential father, tall and rosy-cheeked, who clerks in the office at Building III; two counter clerks who work the canteen, one gray-haired, the other a subaltern-looking shop attendant whom some of the prisoners tease with the threat of going to the front; a hospital orderly who acts a little too familiar and is rather disagreeable. These are the main characters we need to deal with regularly. To a certain degree it depends on us to make those dealings as rare and as short as possible. These Germans are visibly all guided by one thought: they are here, it's a question of remaining here, so you can easily imagine that their zeal is not bent on benefiting us.

At the other end of the hierarchical ladder are the guards, who are probably not the least to be pitied in the whole camp. They are servicemen drafted in the general mobilization, mature men, some skeleton-like, others enormous. One looks like a walking barrel, poor fellow. It's hard not to laugh when you see him. Many do laugh. They are on guard every other day at least, often two days out of three. They are supervised with a violence that amazes even the former adjutants among us, and there are quite a few. It seems that no German warrant officer can give an order without shouting. As everyone knows, in the French army there never existed any warrant officer who shouted or yelled at anyone. All the same, one has to admit that brutality, here among the Germans, is more general, almost systematic. Every morning at ten the changing of the guard takes place before us and we watch it as long as the spectacle presents some novelty, that is to say not for very long. The poor puppets pivot, maneuver, stop, go, and goose-step, under the clearly ironic gaze of the prisoners. They are finally dumped behind the barbed wire zone that they have to patrol, which they do in a melancholy walk. In a little while, at the guard room, they will eat the semolina soup and rutabaga stew or even a sort of mash made from nettles. To stand guard at Mainz is to remain standing outside in all kinds of weather and at all hours, starving, and watching the beaten enemy doing absolutely nothing, sleeping in clean beds, and, relatively speaking, feasting.

For famine does not last. From the middle of 1916 and especially from 1917, the only places where one can eat well in Germany are officer-prisoner camps. We have the right to receive packages in unlimited quantities, therefore the food supplies are now only a matter of money. The rich eat better than the poor. Nothing prevents the well-off from receiving ten pounds of the most sumptuous fare every day. Some have no qualms about doing this and end up collecting large stocks of food. At the end of 1917, when we leave for Poland, some of the French prisoners will take along crates of food supplies weighing one or two hundred pounds. The fear of seeing the package distribution interrupted by reprisals prompts one to stockpile food reserves. It's only sensible.

In the rooms and hallways, everywhere, cooking stoves have been set up where we prepare our real meals ourselves. Official meals at the dining hall are no longer anything but a perfunctory formality, done with in five minutes. Many prisoners don't even show up anymore. Usually each room, or each small group, delegates one or two representatives who pick up what is edible, a few potatoes, a little meat, if there is any, and bring it back to the community mess. The messes organize themselves on the basis of friendship, lasting or disbanding according to the degree of cordiality that exists from within. Often they last a long time. In the summer of 1916, as soon as we receive packages, three comrades and I form one that lasts until the very last days of 1918. Each one in turn does the cooking for a week, and the 'changing of the guard' on Monday morning is often the occasion for an amusing ceremony, unless somebody wants to continue because he enjoys this specialization, which will be my case for a long time. The messes often include men of very diverse financial means and, consequently, whose contribution to the common fund is very unequal. There are misers as well as generous souls. There are also solitary individuals who, either through greed or fastidiousness don't eat with anyone and partake alone of whatever food they have, be it much or little. On the whole, almost everyone ends up eating about twice a day, but there are groups who are perpetually feasting. There is no lack of things to drink. They are part of the packages, and locally, throughout our stay, it will be easier to procure Rhine or Mosel wine or mediocre hard liquors than any tidbit of solid food.[11] The packages rarely get lost, unless the addressee has moved to another camp. Out of about a hundred big weekly packages that were sent to me over two and a half years, all reached me in good condition.[12] Out of another hundred small packages sent through the mail, only three or four didn't arrive. I am filled with admiration and respect when I think that these packages, before reaching me (the enemy), are handled by poor fellows whose bellies are empty and who probably have starving kids at home. Today, I would prefer to think that some of those packages had been stolen.

Each morning they post the list of packages that have arrived. The individuals concerned form a line – this line will be the theme of one of the songs of the 1917 performance – in front of the grated door, which opens at 9:15 a.m. after roll-call. A sentry lets us enter in groups of two or three. In an outbuilding of the *Kommandantur*, in front of the recipients, the packages are opened and carefully examined. A knife is thrust into the bread, sausages are cut in two, bags of beans and lentils are emptied out. We have to bring containers, since they don't give us back the wrappings or any private messages. The pleasant smell of ham and cheese tickles the noses of the inspectors, who for months, soon years, have been living on K rations that include poor quality bread, rotten potatoes, semolina soup, and chopped weeds. Can you imagine this torture, repeated every morning, sometimes for hours at a time? An uninterrupted display of substantial or refined food items passing under the noses of people who eat nothing but garbage, and not even enough of that? This torture, however, is less intense than that of the man in charge of opening canned goods. A can could conceal something, so they must be opened in the presence of a German soldier. Therefore our cans are not given to us directly. Each building has a special cellar in which each prisoner has his own locked trunk. The cans, with our names on labels, are placed in the cellar in these footlockers and carefully guarded. The cellar opens twice a day for half an hour in the morning and in the evening. We go in one by one and get what we want from our chest. An orderly is present, equipped with a whole set of keys and can-openers, and opens the cans under the eyes of the German guard. This poor famished fellow smells, contemplates, and probes the galantines, goose liver stuffed with truffles, chicken in aspic, the best products of Olida and Chevalier-Appert,[13] a benefactor to the human kind, as is printed on all their products, and we do not challenge that statement.

One can see that, in many ways, it was more pleasant to be a prisoner than to be a guard. Were the guards open to bribery? Who would be surprised if they were? I am rather inclined to believe that a few chocolate bars and a few sausages were exchanged for small services, at the expense of stretching the regulations a little. Some members of the French occupation troops in 1919 often boasted that the virtue of a German woman could never resist the lure of a kilo of coffee. I don't believe it was the case in our camp, but the attraction of appetizing products must have been very great for men condemned to eat ersatz products, mostly chemically made. No one, at any rate at Mainz, was ever able to bribe a German sufficiently to persuade him to be an accomplice to an escape.

Naturally, our abstaining from going to the dining hall encourages the German administration to reduce our miserable rations even further. A watchword circulates secretly: we must not spare the enemy in any way. We must demand sternly our due. In particular, we must never give up our weekly loaf of bread which, by the way, we must pay for and which we don't pay for if we don't take it. It is our duty, isn't it, to do everything in our power to starve the enemy. The Germans are furious to find in our stoves half-burned pieces of this bread that their population is starving for.

In spite of the precautions taken, everything enters the camp: civilian clothes, maps, money, and newspapers. Whole packages are pilfered from under the noses of the censors and unopened cans disappear from the cellar. This breech of the rules is because the inspectors are tired of doing their mechanical job, while the thief (who wants his possessions) puts all his energy to use to get what he wants. One swipes not only what is deemed important but anything one can just for the fun of it, for practice. It would be interesting to write a book about all the tricks prisoners use to deceive censorship when they write letters as well as when they receive letters or packages.

From 1917 on, newcomers to Mainz didn't have to suffer the initial famine as harshly as we did. Commanding Officer Raynal had the idea of putting together a food reserve destined to help new arrivals go through the difficult period before they started receiving pack-ages from home. He appealed to the generosity of the earlier pris-oners; it didn't take much to convince them. Donations poured in according to each person's means. I had the honor of being put in charge of the project. In the cellar of our building I kept a large chest, which we had had specially made, filled with canned goods and various food items. I stood next to it during open hours along with the German and French orderlies to serve our new comrades according to how many there were and our resources. When our food supplies were diminishing, I sounded the alarm and called for reinforcements. Within a few days, the chest filled up again. I have to say, and it won't astonish anybody, that not all the beneficiaries remembered later, when they could have, to contribute something in their turn to the treasure that had helped them. Some forgot that, in order to find something in our chest, it was first necessary to contribute to it. The food bank functioned only among the French, essentially because the newcomers were almost all French. Once, a well-intentioned navy officer brought in two British prisoners. I served them without saying anything, but afterwards told their guide that we were not rich enough to feed passers-by, who were gone after a few days and could never help replenish the food supply that had helped them get on their feet again. The German orderly observed all this, and I had some trouble convincing him that the system was based only on goodwill, with no obligation. I told him with some exaggeration that with us everything was done on a voluntary basis, as I remarked in German: '*Bei uns gibt es kein Muss!*' (In our country, there is no 'you must.') In fact, we never ran out of provisions and were always able to help newcomers a little.

Nearby, with no apparent jealousy toward our relative creature comforts, the Russians were suffering heroically. The wealthy among them, or those who had connections in France or England, were receiving provisions in the same way we did, but many were reduced to the official dining room fare. We helped them individually as much as possible. Many of us asked our families to send them packages for which they paid us, if we were not rich enough to simply give presents. Some official organizations helped them a little, but on the whole it is undeniable that they were much more miserable than we were. No, the Allied Forces did not form a solid block against the Germans. There were cracks in the block. The main one came from the fact that the Russians were hungry while the French ate enough. The Belgians lived on the same scale as the French, usually thanks to connections in France or England rather than with their Belgian families, who were starving because of the occupation. What should one have done? Pool together everything that was received by individuals? If we had done so, the 'Allied solidarity' and the 'combatants' fraternity' wouldn't have been empty words. Such common support was impossible to practice and would have satisfied only the individuals who would have benefited from it. Such virtues do not apply to one's belly.

In Mainz, as in all officer camps, there were orderlies, one for six or seven officers, a total of sixty to eighty. None of them had originally been orderlies for the officers they were presently serving. It was by chance that they had come to take on this role, as others worked in the mines or in the fields. The job was far from being a bad one. I never saw anyone voluntarily renounce it among these men, even those who had little natural inclination for the job of servant. Associating with the officers guaranteed decent housing and being safe from brutality. The orderlies' rooms, situated in the attic, were not very different from ours, although there were more inhabitants assigned to each room. The job consisted mainly of housework. Everyone in turn did a training period in the kitchen, which was not without its advantages since, as in any kitchen, and in spite of hard times, the cooks got to eat some choice tidbits. The situation of the orderly depended largely on the group of officers he was serving. These officers' temperaments differed widely depending upon their education and social status, which affected their way of treating servants. In some cases they were like cats and dogs with explosions now and then. In other situations, a real affection united master and servant. The clever orderly received all kinds of financial and dietary benefits from his position. I remember several excellent guys who were true friends for my comrades and myself, and for whom we did everything we could to better their situation. The orderlies answered the roll-call at the same time as the officers but in another area of the courtyard. It was necessary to make sure that one of them did not substitute for an escaped officer. Their usual chief was a German non-commissioned officer with a red beard who claimed to be a Social Democrat and behaved very correctly.[14] The situation of the Russian and Belgian privates was in keeping with that of the French and resembled that of the officers. Of course all these individuals didn't love one another like brothers. The same causes of friction existed among them as among the officers, only there were more of them. I don't see why each one of us (officers) couldn't have made his own bed and swept the room in turn, but we were officers, a fact that most of us, civilians disguised as soldiers, constantly forgot.

The health situation at Mainz was excellent throughout my stay. There were no major illnesses, epidemics or deaths. In fact, any seriously ill prisoner was sent to the city's hospital,[15] from which a convalescent easily escaped one day only to be recaptured shortly afterwards. But even at the hospital, there were no deaths. From the moment of our arrival, all desirable precautions had been taken. Not only were we disinfected, we were also vaccinated. During the first six weeks of my stay, precisely when I was at my weakest, I received six vaccinations, four against typhoid and two against cholera. We explained in vain that we had already been vaccinated against typhoid the previous winter. We had to go through this routine with no exceptions allowed. It was as natural to go and get vaccinated a certain day of the week as it was to go and take a shower another day. The shower room, open every morning for those who love cold water, and one day a week for each building for those who prefer hot water, was, in winter, the stage of comic scenes. We would steal coal in order to increase our meager official rations. When the German orderly, who was walking back and forth, turned his back on the coal pile (destined for the furnace), one, two, or several naked men ran to the heap and grabbed the biggest piece they could find and hurried to hide it under their clothing. We would walk out of the shower room with the coal wrapped in a towel, right under the nose of the guard, a case for court martial. Cold water or hot, everyone was in rather good health. The young, the active, the persevering fought the depression of captivity through physical exercise. Every morning, summer and winter, you could see men in their underwear galloping around the courtyard, a scene we lampooned in our 1917 comic review. For those who preferred more strenuous exercise, there were also parallel bars, a horizontal bar, eighteen-pound weights, and a regular weight. We organized a jumping area in front of Building III. Among 500 men there were necessarily some gymnasts and other athletes. Not content with keeping in shape themselves, they helped and trained the lukewarm sportsmen. A charming and generous classmate from Joinville, Rebillard, I think, never refused to help others with his experience and trained a group every morning.[16] By the spring of 1917, I had regained the thirty pounds of my normal weight and I was in my best physical condition ever. With the assistance of a specialist from Mainz, we managed to set up a tennis court in front of Building II, which from morning to night, weather permitting, was never empty. I caused a lot of harm to my reputation among my friends in France, who until then had felt sorry for me, when I asked for my tennis racket to be sent to me!

Now, we can't spend all our time sleeping, eating and doing gymnastics. One also needs an occupation. I will not repeat all that's been said on the subject but will say a few things that have not been mentioned. The intellectuals, or at any rate those who have an inclination and capacity for studying, learn one, two, three or more foreign languages (often amounting to pidgin) and we read a lot. Through the canteen we can buy anything that does not have too direct a connection with the war, anything that cannot give us dangerous information. One of the town's booksellers sends his catalog to our lending library and even comes and displays his wares, insisting annoyingly on frivolous or lewd books, probably assuming that they will appeal to Frenchmen. The prisoners also write. Many poems, novels or even theses will be brought back from Germany. In a group of 500 men, there are of course teachers of every subject, and a veritable little university is organized. The students rarely cut class. I contribute my little part. The painters paint, the sculptors sculpt, the engravers engrave, the bookbinders bind books. In 1917 we will hold a little exhibition of their work, which is often quite beautiful and interesting. Here and there, everywhere the musicians make music, showing the results of their efforts by giving concerts from time to time. Two choirs perform, one Franco-Belgian, the other Russian. For the individuals who have patience but no creativity there is *kerbschnitt*, which consists of carving with special tools wood ornaments based on ready-made models; there is also *tarso*, which consists of painting and varnishing them in a way that imitates inlaid work. The *kerbschnitter* and *tarso* artists are appreciated by their room-mates because they are silent workers. By contrast, the 'nailer' is not. His art consists essentially of creating designs on wood with a hammer and nails. There is no shortage of those who enjoy netting (embroidery) and tapestry.

Once or twice already I have alluded to less innocent pastimes, which I will now explain. There are circles, often the same ones that have feasts all the time, that engage in serious gambling. There is always a game of roulette going on that attracts a big crowd every afternoon and evening. The bankers get richer, the dupes lose money. There are rooms where poker or baccarat begin immediately after the noon meal, stop briefly for the evening roll-call and dinner, and continue until lights out. When the sentry calls '*Licht aus!*' (lights out), the players emerge from their activities with their brains and faces on fire, discussing their good or bad luck while returning to their rooms. A racetrack type of game also has its addicts. Sometimes the passion for gambling cannot bear to be restrained by the stupid sounding of a clock. The players cover the windows with blankets and continue playing by candlelight – forbidden of course – trying not to make noise because of the sentries. I know some individuals who play this way eight hours a day for years. They play with camp money, zinc coins, which are only accepted inside the walls of the camp. When they don't have any left, they play on their word of honor and write IOUs. I know individuals who returned from captivity with debts of thousands of marks, others with IOUs for equal amounts. Were these 'debts of honor' ever repaid? I don't know.

There are individuals who remain stretched out on their beds the whole day, only getting up for roll-call, if that, and meals.

In a camp there are no women, so chastity is obligatory. How do all these young, robust men manage? Most of them don't talk about it, but many express themselves strongly and crudely (we're soldiers, after all) about the disgrace of such treatment inflicted on us. One guy, a regular Don Juan, known to be particularly afflicted, spends all his time on a reclining chair on the terrace staring at a window of one of the houses we can see and where, from time to time, a woman appears with whom he exchanges signals. By the way, that's all they will ever exchange, unless he returned to Mainz later, as he may well have done. Are there any ersatz substitutes (homosexuals) in the camp itself? It seems very improbable to me, for the very reason that it is impossible ever to be alone, or two people alone. Some do single out a handsome young Russian, a little too pretty and elegant, to whom they give a feminine nickname, but I am convinced that it is slander or a joke. There is one among us, however, who is leading a normal life: Kiki, the dog from Vaux Fort, who has not left Commanding Officer Raynal's side. He is a small dog with long white and red hair, the most popular personality in the camp. He had a serious fight with Von Tecklenburg's Max, but being much the weaker of the two, he came out the loser. Since then, we prevent the two of them from meeting, and all they can do is gallop next to each other, yelling insults, on different sides of the wire fence. But my comrade Felix bought a little black German female dog, and that rascal Kiki, without any patriotic scruple and forgetful of his reputation, had a love affair with the canine enemy and promptly gave her four children. I inherited one of the two allowed to live, and he rapidly became famous in his turn as Nitchevo ('nothing' in Russian), that sad word of despair we all learned very quickly. Lucky Kiki! At least thirty men declared they would like to imitate him.

The main preoccupation of everyone is, of course, the war. We are outside the battle, we live it through communiqués and newspapers, like the bourgeois or retirees in a provincial café. We mark the front on a map with little flags and a piece of string. There are large-scale maps in the library and smaller ones in almost every room. Each room is subscribing collectively to one or several German newspapers, generally the *Frankfurter Gazette* and the *Berliner Tagesblatt* (Daily News). We can also get the *Neue Presse*, from Vienna, and Swiss newspapers, all of which are delivered to us in the morning. In the evening we receive the *Extrablatt* (special supplement), a single red sheet from a Mainz newspaper with the latest bulletins. With this information in hand and if we do the necessary debugging, we know exactly as much as all the so-called 'free' citizens of all the countries in the world. This press contains neither more nor fewer lies than any other; it is only a weapon at the service of the government, just as it is everywhere. The press is complemented by public rumors. Wherever two people are assembled, a rumor begins. In order to believe it, one must be a witness to the innumerable stories, 'tips,' and stupidities that are created, circulated and die among five or six hundred men crammed into two or three hundred square yards for years with nothing to do. One has to cling desperately to what's left of common sense in order not to drown in this sea of gossip. Waves of optimism and pessimism rise, flow over, and submerge everything. Some prisoners claim to be able to decipher the situation by the look on the faces and the attitudes of the German guards who, being only human, are subject to the same influences. What do they know? What we know, what they read in the paper, what everyone knows everywhere. They know what's going on today. But what will tomorrow bring? Neither we nor they know anything about that.

Whenever there is a German victory, all the city's bells ring, flags fly everywhere and it happens often, very often.

We are both compressed and depressed, one being the cause of the other. We get on each other's nerves horribly. In these rooms, you can't take one step toward your bed or a locker or the stove without running into someone. It's mostly at cooking time that one gets jostled. Every gesture must be calculated if you want to avoid collisions; every word must be weighed if you want to keep from hurting someone and provoking reactions that might bring about an altercation. We are horribly tired of each other, our appearances, our faces, our voices, our mental attitudes, our mannerisms. We know each other down to the least nuance of our personalities. It's the test of marriage multiplied by seven, eight, ten, and a marriage in which the couple would be confined to a single room. Superior officers are spared this suffering. Commanding officers are housed by twos, colonels and lieutenant colonels even one to a room. Do they know, will they ever know, how lucky they are? Even when there are only two to a room, I believe there is tension. If we could just each have a single cell! The only way to escape our friends is to walk alone around the courtyard. By being very careful, we can manage to maintain a few yards interval between groups ahead and behind us. It would give me the greatest pleasure in the world, some days, to be able to walk alone, boundlessly, as far as the eye can see on a country road. I have never understood as well as I do at this time the suffering of a bear or a lion in a cage. I don't know whether, intelligent beings that we are, we suffer more or less than they do. There are some among us who run like crazy men. M***, a good-looking, dark-haired, athletic twenty-five-year-old Catalan, runs for hours wearing espadrilles. He has run up to ten miles in an hour around this courtyard. In the spring of 1918 at the camp in Poland where we will be transported, he will throw himself out a window one night just a few days before the authorities permit walks, which would have saved him. He will end up in the hospital with a fractured jaw and a broken arm; we will never see him again after that. He is one of those frantic ones who bang their heads against the wall. One day, from a window of Building III, a Russian prisoner, covered with blood after cutting his wrists with glass from the window pane he has bashed in, throws furniture out, yelling insults to the guard: '*Deutsches Vieh!*' (German cattle!) It takes several men to bring him under control. At the other end of the scale, there are the despond-ent, downhearted prisoners from Liège, Charleroi, and Maubeuge.[17] Very often they just walk around the courtyard, rarely exchanging a few words, in groups of two or three with unshaven beards and lifeless eyes wearing uniforms that already seem to date from another age. To them captivity seems to have gone on forever. It seems that it will go on forever. These guys are really not men anymore; they are almost nothing but prisoners. They no longer believe in anything much or hope for much since they have received nothing but bad news, such as the death of friends and family. They often have no news at all from their families, who remain in occupied countries. Such is the case of about almost all the Belgians. I believe that, when in captivity, one goes through a stage of maximum health, well-being, and balance between six months and a year after capture, when one's body has recovered from the ravages caused by the war. Then collapse sets in for the soul because of the confinement and the feeling of being stifled. The body lacks real exercise (gymnastics and jogging do not replace the freedom to come and go), and the consumption of so much canned food upsets the stomach. From the middle of 1917, I begin my descent like everyone else: I become bitter and weak.

There are, however, rooms where life is a perpetual joke, especially the ones where they eat, drink and gamble a lot. There are few rooms where life is not fun, at times. One may be thirty, forty or forty-five years old and have gray hair, but when one finds oneself in a dormitory, one necessarily, at least from time to time, becomes a schoolboy again, a fresh recruit. All the traditional practical jokes and tricks typical of a dormitory are played all over the place and bring delight to these men who have lived through the most tragic hours of the most tragic times in the history of the world. Almost everywhere, there is a rather naive fellow whom the others like to tease by asking him questions, to which his answers and reactions are predictable, or by making statements or objections that will certainly goad him into irritation. Sometimes it turns nasty. There are puritanical rooms where, when you enter, you can feel the coldness of a chapel. Birds of a feather flock together; we live in clans. There is the Catholic clan, the Protestant clan, the noble clan, the regular army clan, the cavalry, the Southerners, the Corsicans, the former non-commissioned officers, the gunners, the air force clan, the wealthy and many others. One can belong to several or to none at all. Strictly speaking, there is no intellectual clan, intellectuals being by definition all different from each other. The various artistic and sports circles recruit their members everywhere, without reference to clans. But we don't join a clan because we play hockey or tennis with one or several of its members. A special closeness naturally exists between regiment comrades or those who went through the campaign together. A certain solidarity unites those who have a similar educational background. There are never any open conflicts or even any conflicts at all between clans, perhaps because there is no space or reasons for disputes. This is not the struggle for life; there is nothing really worth fighting about. Differences, which are hardly oppositions, become apparent only through a certain ambiance and certain ways of speaking and acting. Unity does not always exist among the individuals (one would think) most likely to get along! Once, in the middle of the courtyard, a colonel slaps the face of a priest. The priests are all interned in officer camps by the Germans, even if they are simply stretcher-bearers, and they have a lot of influence here. Even among them there are clans, such as the Jesuit clan. The general mentality is totally governed by the war. All the talk is about order, authority, reactionary forces and total nationalism. The nationalistic coalition is taking shape. Liberal minds, still able to have a European conscience, are one out of ten, maybe even fewer. Sometimes, in a corner, a theoretical discussion arises between two adversaries, the diehard and the defeatist. The tone rises!

The German territorial guards circulate around this hotbed of opinions with their bayonets at the end of their rifles slung cross-wise. What pitiful creatures we all are, guards and guarded! What are such miserable creatures doing crawling between heaven and earth?

From the patriots' point of view, the good prisoner is the one who annoys the 'Krauts.' From the camp administration's perspective, the good prisoner is the one who, locking himself up in dignity and silence, says nothing, asks for nothing, does not manifest his existence. I am a bad prisoner from the patriots' point of view, a good one for the *Kommandantur*. I happen to be able to write more correctly in German than almost any of us, so I am asked to translate an infinite number of requests, complaints, and protests. What solemn pages I have addressed to the German War Minister to claim lost cans of macaroni or pants confiscated for looking too much like civilian trousers. Those pages would fill a good-sized box, if they could be collected. For that is the way to wage war on the enemy when one is a prisoner, by pestering him to death. The case of E*** in particular gave me a lot of work. He was a graduate of an engineering school, a sugar manufacturer in the department of Oise or Somme.[18] He was condemned to a few months of jail for (being caught in the act) trying to receive or send, I can't remember which, information or objects capable of helping in an escape attempt. He made repeated appeals, which caused the case to drag on for months, even years. He brought me a whole procedure to translate. I became very well versed in the military justice code. I must confess that I no longer remember how the case turned out or whether E*** served in jail or not.

From time to time in the morning a zeppelin flies above us, at low altitude, a magnificent machine, coming back from the front. One day, a great crackling noise and gun fire is heard over Mainz. Very high up, barely perceptible, we see a little white dot that is a French airplane.

The ingenious minds look for ways to escape from here. No one will ever succeed. Hide in a basket of dirty laundry when it is taken to town like Falstaff?[19] Or in a garbage can? It is not feasible here. Everything that goes out of the camp is submitted to a rigorous search. During the first days of my stay, some Englishmen were caught digging a tunnel that started under a platform in the canteen. That tunnel, by the way, would have opened inside the surrounding wall, right below a sentry. The canteen was then moved to the second floor of the kitchen building, and we play billiards there. During the first weeks, it still sold some mediocre wine at modest prices, then wine disappeared or almost. We only go there in the winter, sometimes to steal lumps of coal from the box next to the stove, when the canteen attendant is not looking.

We are not supposed to possess a penny of real money, German, French or any other. Everything that we owned upon arriving, all that is sent to us in money orders, all that we receive as our pay is converted into camp money, which is zinc coins for small sums and brass for larger amounts. Of course it has no value outside the camp. A German worker who came to make some minor repairs and to whom one of us offered a mark as a tip refused it with this delightful phrase: '*Hier est Ihre sogenante Mark!*' (There is your phony mark!) We receive, in accordance with international conventions, half our net pay. The remainder, by the way, will be paid to us when we come home in 1919. For a non-commissioned officer, the net pay is 240 francs per month, half is 120 francs or 96 marks with one mark being worth 1 franc 25 centimes. Since they take out 48 marks for housing(!) and food(!), I end up receiving 48 marks (about $10 at that time). At the end of each month when we file past the treasurer, we can leave all or part of our pay in an account and draw from it according to our needs. It's exactly like a bank but it doesn't pay interest. The redeeming of money orders from France soon provokes a dispute, when the value of the mark starts going down. The German administration ignores this fact, and quite unperturbed continues to give us 81 marks for 100 francs. There is no doubt that they are robbing us and indignation runs high, until the day when some decision or agreement is made. As a result, all earlier money orders are re-examined, the exact difference paid to us, and from then on we are paid according to the day's exchange rate. Did they intend to steal from us? Since then I have seen the French administration take months and even years to realize that the franc had dropped and therefore there were increased postal and telegraphic rates with countries whose exchange rate was high. Would it be possible that 'Madame Administration' in Germany was faster about paying her debts than 'Madame Administration' in France was about claiming her due? That would have been comical.

Christmas 1916: a party for us. The usual three or four groups that eat together unite into one and a single, wonderful feast covers the table. We work busily around our stove in the hallway, in our kitchen aprons, and the same thing goes on pretty much everywhere. There is a lot of joy, drinking and singing. The Germans, guards and employees, are not any less melancholy than usual. In comparison with us, what they eat doesn't improve much, even with the holiday. Nobody, among the Germans nor among ourselves has any illusions about how Wilhelm II's recently published peace offer will be received.[20] I always avoid any private conversation with the camp's staff. I no more want their favor or friendship than I want to 'annoy' them. Being reserved seems to me to be the only proper attitude. That evening, in an empty hallway, I speak for quite a while with the canteen's two employees. They are surprised to hear one of us speaking with moderation and without murdering their language too much. That's all it takes with these simple folk to give me the reputation of being learned and wise. They speak to me directly and trustfully. No doubt about it, Thierry Sandre, they are men and they have a soul. All around our festivities, the sentries continue their pitiful rounds.

Why does Belgium exist as a country? The French-speaking Belgians are Frenchmen, even more similar to the French of the North of France than Northern Frenchmen are to those of Auvergne, Brittany, Provence or the Pyrenees. The Flemish Belgians are Flemish and could live just as easily with us as in the German political system or the Dutch or by themselves. There is never any trace of disagreement between the French and the Belgians. And yet all the Belgians appear to be passionately attached to this recent entity they call Belgium and which did not exist a hundred years ago.[21] They do not have the slightest doubt. It is true that almost all of those who are here are career officers for whom Belgium is their livelihood. As for myself, I keep thinking that the end of the war might well be the end of Belgium. Some of us French look suspiciously at the fat and peaceful Flemish, slow, uncommunicative, eternally smoking their pipes, because they happen to speak a German dialect. Some of them pretend to be violently anti-German, even to the point of avoiding speaking their own language. There may also be among them some 'activists,' more or less secretly pro-German. Most of them wisely keep silent. They know well, because of their own double nature, that German and Welshe are only words, labels applying to the same reference: man.[22]

The winter of 1916–17 is a terrible one, the worst of the war, I believe. Our stealing coal (stealing is a big word for this petty larceny) is excusable. From the windows of Building I, we can see the Rhine carrying enormous ice floes; navigation is at a standstill. The lateral canal to the Main is frozen, and we see skaters on it. Later the Main itself will freeze for a few days. I wake up at dawn in my clean bed, in a warm room, to the sound of all the town bells ringing. I am ashamed thinking about the others, out there at the front.

Sometimes in the middle of the night we are awakened by the sensation of a light shining in our faces. Two or three dark shadows file silently by at the foot of the bed, an electric light flashes held by a gloved hand. It's a check roll-call.

Gloomy spring of 1917: the revolution in Petrograd takes place in March.[23] I foresee and say immediately that Russia won't be with us by the end of the year. I am shamed for being a pessimist and a defeatist. Will this liberating attack never come? It comes, and soon also come our first prisoners, devastated. We feed them. Some only pass through the camp; others remain. Through what surprising accident does a group as large as ours remain together so long in Mainz, which is a temporary camp? We know what happened on the home front. A poorly prepared offensive, rebellions, executions. I never felt so happy to be here. My unit has been hit. If I had still been with it, what would have happened to me? Would I have become the one who shoots or the one who is shot? On the other hand, there is new hope: America is coming to our aid, and Germany is foolishly laughing about it. Brusilov is advancing steadily, but unfortunately stops! Prisoners from his army arrive here. They are no longer the Tsar's guard and army; they are Kerenski's army: officers elected by their own men.[24]

Dear Russian friends, forgive me for taking so long before realizing that you were the most interesting phenomenon in that corner of the world, where one is well placed to meditate on the cruel enigma of our life and universe. Out of the eighteen months I spent in Mainz, I wasted fourteen just rejoicing that I wasn't dead, reconstituting my impoverished body, cooking good things to eat, jumping and running like a colt in an enclosure, a very small enclosure. It's only through contact with you that I woke up again to the life of the spirit, when the animal satisfaction of physical well-being wasn't enough for me any longer and when, belatedly joining many of my comrades, I undertook to learn something about your language and your soul. Your soul? In my turn, I too made my own little discovery of the Slavic soul. For a Westerner, that consists of realizing that your soul is different from ours and is unintelligible to us. East and West will never meet. We are precise, plan ahead, are petty; you are vague, easy-going and generous. We are all more or less clerks sitting behind a counter or a cash register. You are all noble lords. We are puny little trees clinging with all our roots to the soil of a suburban garden. You are leaves carried away by water, clouds blown away by the wind. We are passionately attached to our little life and that makes us realize that others' lives are sacred. You hold yours and theirs superbly in contempt. You treat yours and theirs with splendid cruelty. We know that things are only relatively true, and you believe that some things can be the absolute truth. We are very old; you are very young. Is being old civilization? Then we are civilized and that is not a pretty sight. Is being young barbarity? Then you are barbaric, and that's not a pretty sight either. You have a frightening tolerance for evil and you endure being exploited by all the quacks who claim they will end your suffering, even with swords and fire. You put up with tsars and Bolsheviks. After all, your patience is perhaps only another form of resignation. I wonder if you don't think, as I do (I happen not to be a typical 'Westerner') that the sole supreme consolation in front of evil is that evil will end when man ends. Friends, we don't understand each other; our brains have nothing in common. I have not met a single one of you whose mind functions as mine does. But where do individual characteristics end and national traits begin? I don't understand you, yet I love you. There are nations and individuals whom I understand but don't like.

My friend and Russian language professor is Andreiev, a good-looking, thirty-year-old man, medium sized, vigorous and well built with blue eyes and a blond moustache. He could well appear in geography textbooks representing the perfect type of the Caucasian race, next to the black, yellow, red and classic South Sea Islander races. He was a Cossack officer in the region of Semipalatinsk on the border of Turkestan and from there he left to go and invade Prussia in August 1914. A photo on his table shows him leaning against a young woman standing next to him, his wife. I often notice that in that photo, he has a strange expression, with his eyes sort of blinking. One day I venture to ask him the reason. He gives it to me good-humouredly, and without embarrassment! It was the day his regiment was leaving, so they had been drinking a lot. His wife wanted a photo, since she didn't have one. He was drunk, and she was holding him up to prevent him from falling over. Everyone can see the photo, and he explains it with simplicity. If a Westerner knew that there existed such a picture of him, he would go and set fire to the house of the photographer who took it in order to destroy the negative. Andreiev is the gentlest, most charming companion with the best manners I have ever come across in my life. I have never seen him other than smiling and full of exquisite courtesy. He appears to have lost all hope and has abandoned all intentions of ever rejoining his wife and going back to leading his Cossacks. He wants to become a business clerk in London or New York! And this is why, on alternate evenings, I teach him English and he teaches me Russian. But the textbook we use is not business-like at all. It is *The Portrait of Dorian Gray*, a work for which Russians have boundless admiration. They recognize in Oscar Wilde the most Russian and the least English of all Englishmen, and rightly so, in my opinion.

Andreiev shares a little room in the attic of Building II with only two room-mates; they are privileged in this way. One of them, Rink, from the Baltic States, is handsome, young, elegant, and always with a mysterious smile. He speaks French, English, and German equally well. What does the constantly courteous, refined, gentle and cultivated young man really think? I believe he is skeptical because of the intermingling inside him of various languages and motherlands. The other room-mate, Nelukov, is a pope who, one has to admit, is dirty: dirty hair, dirty beard, dirty clothes. He doesn't know a word of any Western language and doesn't seem to speak with anyone ever, even with the Russians. When I am present, which perhaps he dislikes, he does not even talk to his room-mates. Once a week, he makes a trip to Worms to the Russian soldiers camp we saw in passing to bury the week's dead, fifteen, twenty, twenty-five, depending on how many they let accumulate until his arrival. It is through him that we learn about the terrible suffering of these miserable creatures. What can these handsome young men (Andreiev and Rink) think about Christianity as represented by Nelukov?

Late in the afternoon, I leave them to go have a dinner so superior to theirs that I always avoid that topic, and I rejoin them afterwards until lights out. We never talk about the present phase of the war and ways to put an end to it. The phenomenon is beyond our comprehension. We may as well talk about preventing Vesuvius from smoking.

The most well-known Russian in the camp is Miloradovitch. He is almost seven feet tall, broad-shouldered in proportion to his height, and immensely strong. He is from the Guard and is a rich landowner in Little Russia.[25] Needless to say, he speaks French and, less well, English. He speaks with a mean smile about the events of 1905 and about the machine guns opening fire on the crowd.[26] He seems to be the head of the noble and reactionary group in the camp, at least among the young ones for there are also mature men up to the rank of colonel, all of them characters out of Tolstoy. But at the other end of the scale, and apparently without links other than simple politeness with the other group, are characters from Dostoyevsky. There is a studious man, who for years has been seen with his nose in a book. Short-sighted, he holds it very close to his eyes twelve hours a day, even when he is walking. There is also a remarkable musician who attracts crowds at night around the rented piano in the hallway of Building II. The Russian choir rehearses every day. When we give a concert together, we French and Belgians perform first; after the Russians we would appear ridiculous. During the morning shower I notice some admirable sculptural bodies; there are also some old syphilitic men!

What is going on among these comrades? The March revolution has divided them deeply. The partisans of the old regime don't even look at the prisoners from the Brusilov offensive, when they start arriving in the camp. In their eyes, these men are not officers; they have betrayed the Tsar. They are a curious mixture: some are half or three-quarters peasants; others are Russians from the Boulevard St. Michel or from Geneva.[27] Chatilov, to whom I immediately have packages sent from Paris, has studied medicine in Paris. He is the most desperate man, the darkest pessimist I have ever known. Our prisoners from Maubeuge are cheerful compared with him. He is ghastly pale with a stubble of beard, looking like a statue of sadness in his poor yellowish overcoat. From the outside, the Russians seem to pass by without seeing each other. They salute or speak only if there is no way to avoid it. They don't talk to us about the schism; we are friends but foreigners. We might not know how much each group hates the others. We only know that a 'twenty-three group' has formed among the most determined revolutionaries. One day, through my beginning knowledge of Russian, I gather the general meaning and some specific snatches of a violent discussion. Then suddenly we learn that a group of Russians is leaving for a reprisal camp, but I can't remember why. They say the camp is very small, built on piles near a mosquito-infested bog. To go on this trip, the administration chooses on the one hand 'the twenty-three group' and on the other the leaders of the Old Russia group. We will not see them again. Were they devoured by mosquitoes or by each other? Or did they simply starve to death?

On July 14, 1917, we hold a celebration. Every Sunday we air out our best uniforms and put on our decorations, if we have any. We also celebrate in this way the independence of Belgium, the birth of King Albert, Holy Russia, and any important success of the Allied Forces.[28] It is rare; a password circulates from room to room: 'full-dress uniform; all flags flying.' It's our way of answering the town's displays of flags and gun salutes. But July 14 is naturally the most important day of the year, and the one that justifies maximum solemnity. Early in the morning, the oldest Russian and Belgian officers – the nation's most ancient, as the Germans call them – pay an official visit to the oldest among us, a very diplomatic gesture. Last year there were too many of us famished newcomers for the festivities to be very joyful. This time, there is an over-abundance of food supplies, therefore the ambiance is warmer. A veritable international sports competition is planned for several days. Classic distances to be run: 100 meters (reduced to about 80 meters for lack of space) diagonally across the courtyard; 400 meters, 1,500 meters, and even 5,000 meters by running behind Building II; a hurdle race with the benches as hurdles; high jump (long jump being impossible for lack of space); and a weightlifting competition using the only bar and raising it as many times as possible. In the competition among the orderlies, a Russian peasant, thickset and of average size, fed on weeds and rotten potatoes, wins by far over every exploit accomplished by well-nourished officers. There are relay races between the three nations; gymnasts show their talents on the horizontal bar and the parallel bars; a great tennis tournament is held. During the whole competition, betting goes on under the direction of an expert bookie.

The Russians do not usually shine much during all these events. In order to run, one has to be able to eat, and the melancholy walk which they, more lucky than us, take outside once a week, does not constitute sufficient training. I do my small part by placing fourth out of four in the 100-yard race. True, two of the others are first in the finals.

I believe it is around that time that Pastor N*** begins to explicate Goethe's *Faust* for us. Yes, there is in Mainz a man, a minister of the Christian religion, who happens to think that the men imprisoned up there in the Citadel are men, that tomorrow they will not be enemies any longer, that their minds are open to great masterpieces and to the bright lights of the human spirit. It's also likely that he wants to show us that 'Germans are not barbarians,' and he is quite right. There is no doubt that the German authorities look favorably on what they consider good propaganda. To me, it is absolutely certain that the intentions of this decent man are pure and noble and he is acting on his own initiative. Yes, here is a man who stresses what can unite rather than divide. And there are many among us, my extremist brothers, a good number of simpletons (about twenty or thirty) who fall into this trap, surely set for us perfidiously, don't you think, by German duplicity. Not just intellectuals, but officers from the regular army and even a staff officer.[29] Of course, some only consider this session as an opportunity to learn German, but the fact that they attend is a victory in itself. For the most part, they are perfectly capable of meeting and absorbing the great thoughts presented here. Our professor's tact and refinement are impeccable. The class meetings are rarely anything but a monologue on his part. Few of us could express ourselves sufficiently well to discuss such a topic, and those who could say something don't want to. As for myself, faithful to my custom of not looking for any personal contact with our guards, I always sit at the back of the classroom and never open my mouth.[30] The explication of *Faust* by N*** is OK, not sensational. Not so many years ago, one of my professors, Godard, gave us a much more pithy commentary, but N's is perfectly clear, leaving in doubt no aspect of the language or thought. You might ask, is this possible? Out there on the battlefield men of the two races are murdering each other while here the minds of both races meet over the words of a philosopher. I don't know whether it is possible; I do know that it is a fact. I don't even believe that anyone in the camp is looking askance at us for dealing with the enemy. It's only a lesson in German. Goethe and *Faust* are of no concern to most prisoners, even if they have heard about them, which is not the case for everybody. Pastor N*** inspires absolute trust in all who come in contact with him. When we leave the camp, we will give him, as a token of our gratitude and as a memento, a beautiful art book with a short dedication and our signatures. I imagine he will keep it and will recognize himself, if he reads this.

A few days later, the great summer pantomime show takes place. Several times, to accompany Sunday afternoon concerts, we perform sketches and short comedies, but this time the actors are not flesh and bones; they are paper or cardboard silhouettes cleverly drawn and painted and held up by wooden sticks. They walk in procession on the little stage similar to a puppet theater set in a recess between Building II and the courtyard. Several voices speak and sing the text. The theme is a day at the Mainz camp, from reveille, with athletes very scantily dressed who trot around the terreplein until lights out. The grand finale is a dream about after the war when we all file past dressed in civilian clothes. All the important characters of the camp get hauled over the coals with their idiosyncrasies and absurdities. Of course no German appears, except for a 'neutral' character, easily recognizable for us and whom the censors overlook, voluntarily or not. The silhouettes are incredibly true to life, the text is bright and witty, and the songs very cleverly written. I still remember some and sing them now and then. There are songs about gymnastics, Kiki (the mascot of Fort Vaux), the Spanish ambassador who was supposed to defend our rights, and a song that makes fun of the gaudy elegance of one of our comrades. Some of the lampooned comrades only force a laugh. I have the honor of appearing in the show. My silhouette, which I will bring home with great care, exaggerates my air of being miles away, my indifference about being fashionable, and the extreme casualness of my everyday dress. The portrait is particularly striking since I willingly posed for the caricaturist. The conversation that my silhouette is having with my friend B*** is a take-off on my slow delivery, pompous tone, and my imperturbable calm and wisdom. On the whole, they haven't savaged me too badly; many others are mistreated more than I am. The authors, by the way, (there are lots of them) don't spare each other. The text is full of allusions to the enemy and to the camp personnel, references that go unrecognized by the Germans. But we don't get on our high horse and discuss the war between civilization and barbarity. We make a few jabs at most. Some censorship employees watch the show from a distance among the standing audience, comprehending very little. There is not much to understand; nothing very nasty is said in the show.

My dog, Nitchevo, in spite of his shameful origins, is becoming extremely popular, almost as much as his famous father and much more than his brother Tchiorni, 'Blackie,' which F*** has kept and whom Nitchevo outshines in vigor and playfulness. Nitchevo is a totally black little creature with a white spot on his chest and short, sleek hair. Because he whimpered non-stop the first night he was away from his mother, all my room-mates wanted to kill me, and I thought for awhile that I would have to get rid of him, but he soon adapted and sleeps quietly in a box under my bed. The deposits he leaves along the hallways (he too is locked up at least twelve hours a day) cause some trouble for me with the *Kommandantur*, but it's nothing compared with the joy he gives everybody in the camp. I try in vain to feed him sensibly, but everyone stuffs him full of cookies and sugar, which actually don't appeal to him as much as certain garbage cans he has discovered in a corner. Some of my friends let him loose in front of mice they have caught in traps in the attic and everyone marvels at seeing him learning his hunting skills. French, Belgians, Russians or Germans can't pass by without stopping to pet him. No one can resist the charm and clumsiness of a young animal, just like no woman can resist a young baby. A little dog, a little child, they don't have a motherland.

When there are seven or eight men in a room, there is always one who snores. We throw shoes at him, shake him and wake him up, but he swears he doesn't snore.

In a room, there are always two factions, those who want the window open and those who prefer it closed. Because of this conflict, men have broken relationships which had endured for months, even years. Because of this disagreement, men have sometimes actually had physical fights. The Russians are usually on the side of closed windows. I imagined that these Northmen rolled around naked in the snow. They are actually the people most sensitive to cold on earth; they live all bundled up.

On August 10, 1917, the Mainz camp loses an important part of its population. The idea is to establish in Trier a new camp which will receive its equal share of the bombs the Allied Forces are dropping on the city's population.[31] A group of French and Belgians leaves, 100 or 150, the largest departure since I have been here. What principle dictated who would leave? It's impossible to say. Friends are separated and long-standing eating groups are broken up. I myself lose some very dear friends. A veritable column forms and sets out from under the great entrance, surrounded by German infantrymen with loaded weapons. But the members of the column are no longer a pitiful sight; everyone is loaded down with packages and bundles, and some large baggage will have to be put on wagons.

'Nothing ever happens in your story! It's boring.' Well, nothing happens but it's not boring, it's terrible.

Throughout the sinister summer of 1917, anguish has us by the throat. Rumania attacks Austria and soon the bells ring for the capture of Bucharest. It does seem to us as though we cannot be beaten, the Hohenzollern can no longer become masters of the world; France will not be broken to pieces, life will start again, we will find again our places in civil society, in peace. But when? How? A large dark cloud hides the future. I become depressed again. I find myself telling those who complain that maybe one day we will regret the comfort we are presently enjoying, our security, our relative certainty about tomorrow. I was wrong for us Westerners, but oh, my Russian comrades, how many of you will have found in 'freedom' a destiny worse than this prison! If one is capable of distancing oneself a little from the situation, of closing one's eyes to the proximity and over-abundance of one's fellow humans, it is possible to be relatively happy here. Considering what happiness is, I have been relatively happy here. In the camp one can improve the body and the mind, and we're sheltered from women's snares. I ironically invite the complainers to seize the opportunity to become 'as handsome as Alcibiades and as wise as Plato,' and sure enough, in the show they have my silhouette say this line.[32] But if there was in Tartarin a domestic rabbit and a wild rabbit, there is inside each human being the dog and wolf of La Fontaine's fable.[33] The dog can be content; the wolf suffers if he is tied up. Each day the dog becomes less satisfied and the wolf suffers more. There are days when I hate everyone around me. Ah, if only we could each have a cell! Those who are sent to a cell as punishment for something come back physically pale and weakened because of being deprived of food other than official fare but they are mentally appeased.

The more time passes, the darker the horizon. Every morning I spend an hour with Commanding Officer Raynal, whose reading knowledge of German is poor and for whom I summarize the newspapers. It's all out submarine warfare, England is put on short allowance, France is barely recovered from her deep depression, Kerenski and Brusilov's efforts have been stopped, the second revolution and, therefore, the Russian defection are in the works.[34] In the background, America is arming herself. Will she make it here in time?

There is one way to get out of here: internment in Switzerland, which was instituted at the beginning of the war for sick prisoners, especially those with lung problems. There are two ways of being interned in Switzerland. The first is to be seriously ill, and fortunately I can't claim that one. The second is to be rich and powerful, and that is just as impossible for me. No one will ever know how much this hope of being transferred to Switzerland has caused ink to flow, inspired visits and canvassing, maneuvering, and plotting in all of Western Europe. The Swiss delegations that periodically visit the camps in search of the 'sick' are overwhelmed with recommendations that arrive through the most distant and distorted ways. Churches and the world of finance are quite clever when it comes to making friends among the enemy jailers. I am not accusing Swiss doctors of favoritism and being susceptible to bribes, but I am saying, and everyone knows it, that influence and money play a considerable role in selections for being assigned to a Swiss medical facility. Many of those who were admitted died in Switzerland; many have trouble remembering today the reason given to send them there. After all, in order to extract a prisoner from his prison, all the doctor has to do is to declare that captivity is harmful to him. I would like to know for whom it is beneficial! The visit of a delegation is a considerable event, much talked about in advance, and for which the candidates for a medical reassignment prepare themselves through all means known to draftees who are not very enthusiastic about doing their military service. In an effort to qualify to be sent to a Swiss medical facility, you deprive yourself of food and sleep and throw your heart out of rhythm by excessive violent exercise and excessive consumption of coffee. You present yourself with an unshaven beard and a pasty complexion. Add to that some powerful friends in Geneva or Bern and you have a chance. The rejected applicants come out of the interview furious; the happy 'sick ones' are beside themselves with joy. Some are even arrogant in their good fortune while even the strongest of the non-candidates are secretly jealous. Alas, there are some unfortunate prisoners who don't need to pretend to be sick in order to leave.[35]

A more frankly comical performance is the periodical visit of the little Spanish embassy secretary who comes to hear our grievances, since Spain, truly diplomatic, has been in charge of French interests since the Franco-German break in relations. The Spanish representative is some insignificant young man whom the camp authorities monopolize as soon as he arrives and show around officially, leading him to admire the excellent perfection of everything, keeping him at a safe distance from the prisoners. It is forbidden to approach 'His Excellency's representative' as the summer show calls him, and it is in vain that some try to hand him petitions when he walks by. But at a given time, he receives anyone who wants to talk to him. The conversation takes place in French, in the presence of the administration. One of us who can speak Spanish interprets, but the truth is that he has nothing to say. What could all these whiners ask for? Lost packages, confiscated clothing, basically, trifles. Keep in mind that one must 'pester the Krauts.' Their main grievance is that they are prisoners, and the Spanish ambassador can't do anything about that. He can't do much either about the specific requests that are presented to him. Generally, there is no follow-up. Whoever is in charge makes proper notes and the affair is 'in progress,' as the classic phrase goes. A few days after the visit, a superb civilian wearing a fatigue-jacket turned inside out, a straw hat, paper wrist cuffs, and a monocle and carrying a walking stick walks the prescribed route in front of the astonished sentries. It's a practical joker pretending to be the Spanish embassy's secretary.

We think that the earlier closing of the buildings, due to the approach of fall, comes too early. It deprives us of half an hour of outside air and light. When two Corsican protesters manage to remain outside alone after closing, the Germans stick them in jail for a few days. That will give them a change as a distraction.

I hear a lot of people around me say that after the war we will be 'wiser'; everyone agrees about that. But for some, it means that nations will stop arming themselves against one another because the arms race leads to war. For others, it means that they will arm themselves much more because we weren't armed enough and that is why we were attacked. As for myself, I believe, and I am even sure, that they are all correct.

Winter arrives this year like the shadow of death for our bruised and embittered souls. In summer, at least, we can tolerate things and people. We're inside only during a minimum number of hours. But when the doors open later and close earlier, we are more and more thrown together and for fourteen, then fifteen, then sixteen hours, our life is enclosed in the stifling atmosphere of the dorms. We cannot have any doubts about it anymore. We will not get out of prison this year. How many more years will we be here? My mental equilibrium is broken. I am wasting away and becoming bitter. Others notice it.

The second Russian revolution at the beginning of November only surprises those who did not want to see it coming. We don't talk about it with my Russian friends. What could we say about it? We peacefully continue studying the language and the life of the Tsars' Russia. There is no doubt that the new Russian leaders are going to make a deal with Germany; the negotiations begin almost immediately, and soon the rumor is that the French and Belgians will be totally evacuated from the camp, leaving only the Russians here. Since they will no longer be at war with Germany, they cannot be subjected to the same treatment as we are. Rumors about departure have circulated so often that this evacuation plan is met at first with some suspicion. But soon doubt is no longer possible and we receive the official order to be ready to leave the camp by December 7, 1917.

Notes

1. In 13 B.C. Drusus, stepson of Emperor Augustus, erected a fortified camp on the site of modern-day Mainz.

2. In *Au-dessus de la Mêlée* Romain Roland wrote: 'The idols of race, or of civilization, or of Latin culture, which they [French intellectuals] consider so important, don't satisfy me. I don't like any idol, even the idol of Humanity' (p. 92).

3. The Taunus Mountains (2,816 feet) and Wiesbaden, one of the main cities of the province of Hesse, are within thirty miles of Frankfurt and Mainz.

4. Marshal Vauban was known as a builder of fortresses. Louis XIV put him in charge of fortifications in 1678; many French cities still have remains of his impenetrable defense structures. Vauban was also a master in the art of besieging enemy citadels.

5. Mons and Charleroi are two Belgian cities situated six and twelve miles from the French border and about thirty miles from Brussels. In August 1914, the French and British armies had to fight violent battles in these towns after Liège was captured.

6. Marshal Kitchener (1850–1916). In the Franco-British rivalry for the colonization of Central Africa, Kitchener, allied with Egypt, got the upper hand in Sudan in 1898. In South Africa he won the Boer War, annexing the provinces of Orange and Transvaal. In 1914, though retired, he organized British volunteers to help France. He died while on board a ship that was destroyed by a torpedo.

7. Sadowa. In July 1866 the Prussian army was victorious over the Austrian army, which definitively ended the rivalry between the two greatest states of the German Empire. From then on, Prussia was the leading power and around it, under the leadership of Chancellor Bismarck, the unity of Germany was achieved.

8. Tétaud was Connes's former classmate at the *École Normale Supérieure*.

9. German *Kommisbrot* (army bread) was made from rye. The French jokingly called it *caca* bread (poop bread).

10. Polichinelle is the French equivalent of puppet Punch.

11. Mosel wines, from the vineyards of the Rhine and Mosel region, are famous.

12. Sending these packages must have amounted to quite an effort for Connes's parents. Connes had gone to college on a scholarship, and his father was a modest postal employee.

13. Olida and Chevalier-Appert are two famous trademarks for meat products. Olida still exists. In 1852 Chevalier-Appert invented a hermetically-sealed cooker that allowed food to be preserved when the temperature rose to 212°F.

14. For decades socialism had been gaining ground in Germany, opposing the ever autocratic and dominant forces. In the election of 1912, the socialist party became the largest. Social Democrats were the most influential and moderate of the socialists. They were against the war.

15. Captain (later to become General) Charles de Gaulle was wounded and captured on March 2, 1916 and treated at the Mainz hospital.

16. Rebillard was a former classmate at the Joinville Normal School of Gymnastics and Fencing. Joinville-le-Pont, a town on the Marne River west of Paris, is where the students of the *École Normale* traditionally did part of their military service.

17. Maubeuge is a French city on the Belgian border where hard battles were fought in 1914 after Liège was captured by the Germans.

18. Oise and Somme are departments north of Paris.

19. Falstaff is a character who appears in several of Shakespeare's plays. He is the witty and amoral companion of Prince Hal.

20. As the war progressed, Germany was encountering mixed successes, more economic problems and growing opposition at home. As a result, Germany made several attempts at peace proposals, all of which failed until November 1918.

21. Belgium became independent in 1830 and an official country in 1831. Until then its various provinces had been under the control of Austria, Spain, France, and the Netherlands.

22. Welshe or velche was the derogatory term used by Germans to refer to any population speaking Latin-related languages, especially French and Italian.

23. On March 11–12, 1917, the Russian revolution took place in Petgrograd and Tzar Nicolas II abdicated. From that point on, Russia's support of the Allied Forces greatly diminished.

24. In the summer of 1917, Alexei Brusilov (1853–1926), commander-in-chief of the Russian army for a time, led powerful and victorious attacks against the Central Powers (Austria, especially), but he was eventually forced to stop for lack of equipment. Alexander Kerenski (1881–1970) was a socialist who became temporary head of the Russian government and tried to continue helping the Allied Forces but was eventually overthrown by Lenin's Bolsheviks, who didn't want to continue the war.

25. The term 'Little Russia' was often used to designate the region of Ukraine as opposed to 'White Russia' (now Belarus) and 'Great Russia,' the northern and central parts of the former Soviet Union.

26. Against the repressive regime of the tsars, revolutionary and nihilistic movements had grown since the middle of the nineteenth century and were always crushed. In 1904 and 1905, agitation, strikes, and assassination attempts increased and were put down by a great massacre. These events are often called the first Russian revolution and they weakened absolutism.

27. Not only was there a political schism between Russian conservatives and Russian liberals, but also at this time of intense intellectual life (the time of Pouchkine, Gogol, Turgenev, Dostoyevsky, and Tolstoy), between those who thought that everything from Western Europe was evil and those who welcomed it as capable of contributing richly to the regeneration of Russia. The latter are probably those Connes calls 'Russians from the Boulevard St. Michel or from Geneva.'

28. Holy Russia was the motto of the conservatives in Russia, especially Tsar Nicolas I. Russia had to be preserved from Western European influences and return to its Slavic origins.

29. Connes is being ironic here.

30. During the German occupation of France during the Second World War, Connes totally refused cultural contacts with the enemy, which were systematically organized by the Nazis.

31. Trier is a German city on the Mosel River near the Luxemburg border.

32. Alcibiades (450–404 B.C.) was extremely handsome but very dissipated, a total contrast with Plato (428–347 B.C.), who was ugly but very wise.

33. In Alphonse Daudet's novel *Tartarin de Tarascon* (1872) the protagonist has two opposite traits: he is at once a super-brave hero and a rather stay-at-home, comfort-loving character. In La Fontaine's fable 'The Wolf and the Dog,' the wolf at first envies the comfortable life of the domestic dog, well-fed with nothing to do, but eventually realizes that he wouldn't accept the price the dog has to pay: being tied up.

34. The reference here is to the major revolution, which started in March 1917.

35. Connes was annoyed by the fact that Thierry Sandre did not explain how or why he was liberated after only nine months of captivity. Without

mentioning Sandre's name, Connes suggests in this paragraph that having connections or pretending to be sick could result in a prisoner being sent to a hospital in Switzerland. See Annette Becker, *Oubliés de la grande guerre*, to understand the mechanism of repatriation and 'humanitarian diplomacy.'

4

Eastward Bound

Where are we headed? We are not supposed to know, but after conflicting rumors, truth finally filters through to us: we are heading for a town in western Prussia whose name is dear to us, according to an employee of the *Kommandantur*. We soon find out that there is a Strasburg in that province, which is, indeed, our destination.[1] The fact is known and accepted several days before our departure. Our emotions are divided between the joy of change with a trip and regret for the comfort and habits we have created here. We are familiar with what we are leaving behind but we don't know what to expect ahead. We probably won't find much of anything. It appears that we are not going to simply join a fully functioning camp but rather a new camp that is just being set up. Therefore, we expect to find nothing. Indeed we will find nothing and, to make matters worse, we are moving further away from France, eastward, toward uncertainty and fear. When and how will we get back? Won't it be more difficult to get out of here when the end comes? This is a fear that the future will justify also.

We arrived in Mainz like beggars; we leave loaded with all the treasures of the earth. When we were leaving Stenay, all we had to do was get up and go. Now we will need several days to prepare for our departure. This is not a transfer of prisoners. It is the moving out, the migration of a village with its baggage and furniture. We are, naturally, taking along all that belongs to us, and some of us have accumulated a considerable amount of goods. A whole train is formed for us and no limits are imposed as to weight, number or size of our luggage. By now everyone owns trunks and suitcases, loaded with supplies of food. There are pieces of furniture that some prisoners have made or bought, including tables, chairs, garden furniture, and lawn chairs. Almost every dorm is taking along one or two cooking stoves with the attached pipes. We in our room have a very old worn-out stove we packed carefully and which will survive the trip relatively well. We and many others have a whole, recently

77

purchased supply of firewood forwarded. The kitchen utensils alone would fill a whole car. It takes several trips to the train station to transport all the crates of canned goods brought up from the special storage bins in the cellar. After packing and sending the big baggage, we don't even have enough hands to carry all the little packages.

The column has formed in the courtyard, which is our gathering point for departure. Here we are waiting for the signal to get started, standing or sitting on our suitcases, overloaded with packages, warmly dressed in our best uniforms, all cheered up at the thought of seeing the other side of these walls. We look like a bunch of immigrants, but wealthy immigrants. There is no scarcity of pets. Kiki, Tchiorni, and Nitchevo are tugging at the ends of their new leashes, purchased especially for the occasion. There are numerous cats in baskets, birds, and even a superb parrot in a cage. One fellow is content with a small stuffed bear, which he carries under his arm. Captain Von Tecklenburg, who is to accompany us as far as Poland, walks back and forth along the column to make sure everything is ready. On our right and left, he positions the traditional lines of foot soldiers, young men who, according to the classic and symbolic gesture, load their weapons in our presence and for our benefit. That's it. Von Tecklenburg raises his arm and the gates open. Farewell, Mainz Citadel! You have weighed heavily on me for so long. Mainz Citadel, I don't hate you. When I was imprisoned within your walls, I was younger and still had many illusions.

Farewell, Russian friends, you who are watching us leave with so much sadness and whom we will never, ever see again. We feel that you are deeply ashamed, and even those of you who support the men in Moscow are not without sadness. Not one of us, not even the ones who are furious, have the courage to say one word of reproach to you, so only gestures and words of friendship are exchanged. This separation, which is forever, tears something out of our hearts, even for those of the camp's most intellectual and intelligent individuals, who, having recognized much earlier than the first revolution all that is indefinite and immeasurable in your souls, called you 'the Moscow barbarians.' Even for those who, like me, know that coming from you, children of the Orient, one must expect nothing but one must be ready for anything. We who are unfortunately clear-sighted are those who love you the most. What became of you? Miloradovitch, did you fall victim to one of your peasant's bullets or knives? Andreiev, did you perish in Siberia in the ranks of some snow-covered army? Did you achieve your dream of becoming a bureaucrat in some bank in London or on Wall Street? Old white-haired colonels, are you rotting away in the squalor of some low-rent housing for old folks in Marseilles? Are you dying away in some Sisters of Charity hospice? Gloomy Chatilov, are you a commissioner of something somewhere and have you ordered a murder in the pursuit of the ideal? Russian friends, I think of you and I see Frenchmen who have not lost a son, brother or husband in the war and yet complain of having suffered in this tragedy.

We leave the Citadel at Mainz. This is not the way we had hoped to come out. A light snow covers the ground as we go down the steep path leading to the south train station. I walked up this path exactly a year and a half ago. It's so cold that no one in town bothers to come and watch us. They have seen it all before and are totally occupied with their quest for daily bread. Only a few friendly children trot along and chat with us. 'Super-patriots' are right to teach children hatred of the person who dresses differently and speaks another language, for hatred does not come naturally to children. This is curious and unexplainable from the patriotic point of view, but when a Frenchman and a German woman, or when a German male and a French woman get together, a little human can be born.

The loading proceeds rapidly and in an orderly fashion. We are well treated. There are first- and second-class cars in sufficient number. There is no shoving, and they let us group ourselves as we wish. With my three faithful mess buddies – and Nitchevo! – the five of us occupy the comfortable seats of a first-class compartment. The sentries don't come in with us but remain in the corridor. Before opening the door to see what's going on, they knock on the compartment window like a conductor who comes to check tickets! The next day I will talk at length with one of the guards. He is like me, nothing but a poor guy who suffers and doesn't understand. As the whistle blows, we cast one last look through the window at the Citadel. We are on our way! We soon cross the bridge over the Rhine and, for the first time, realize how huge the river is and the bridge that spans it. Viewing the Rhine from the hill above, we didn't have a real sense of its size. We are rolling eastward up the Main valley and then, a couple of hours after our 2 p.m. departure, night falls hiding everything. With the darkness comes the terrible cold. The heating system doesn't function well; some pipe must be frozen. We walk up the train following the corridor, looking for a better temperature in neighboring cars. There we find another problem: stifling heat and people taking off everything down to their shirts. In our car it was like Siberia; here it is Senegal and the cold-blooded passengers congregate in a horrible pile-up. In the end, we prefer to return to our Siberia. We stretch out two by two on each seat, head facing toes. Nitchevo finds his place between my friend Guintrand and myself, and his little body radiates heat in this ice-house. In spite of blankets and coats, we shiver for about twelve hours, one of the cruelest nights of my life. The temperature must be 15 or 20°F; there seems to be no difference between outside and inside. We will take a while to realize that morning has come. There is half an inch of ice on the window panes, and it will not melt away during the day. About noon, somewhere in Saxony, Von Tecklenburg manages to have the heating system fixed. With the help of lamps, the frozen pipe is thawed and soon there is neither Siberia nor Senegal but rather a pleasantly temperate climate. 'Well-informed' people explain that Von Tecklenburg's zeal comes from the fact that he himself froze all night. We have a picturesque stopover in a little station for this repair to be made. We get off the train in order to watch the repairmen and to stretch our legs, but the guards are vigilant and would shoot at the slightest attempt to escape.

The country we are traveling through bears the marks of the gigantic effort of a nation that doesn't want to die. Everywhere there is work in progress, on the land and in factories. Even the fiercest enemies of Germany among us are silent, impressed by this sight. In comparison, France, when one travels through it by train, looks like a wild and deserted land. Toward the end of the afternoon, we circle around Leipzig,[2] which reminds me of American cities with its carefully laid out new districts, and where only about a tenth of the space is already inhabited. I don't think the population of Leipzig is one million. There is room for three or four million just in the space available for building, without the need for one new street, and the railroad appears to be up to par with the city. The train viaducts cross over boulevards. Since the train goes slowly, we have time to catch glimpses of life in the suburbs, which resemble those of any large city. Seeing women moves us. Every square yard of land produces vegetables. Railway workers cultivate little garden plots wherever the soil is able to produce anything and they also raise rabbits, which the Germans scorned doing before the war. It's a sign of changing times. Night-time approaches and no food has been provided to us today. We consume the provisions that had been supplied when we left, or rather we don't consume them for they are inedible, but we all have our own provisions.

Passing through Weimar this morning was a moving experience for some of us.[3] The first night was the night of the cold; this one is the night of the snow. It is coming down thick, and the darkness around us is white. Sometimes the train stops in the middle of nowhere, but no one knows why. We open the window a little, and the light from our compartment produces a dazzling white square on the embankment. Beyond it, one guesses that the white country-side extends to the horizon. All is deadly silent. At this moment, it would be the easiest thing to jump to the ground. That small leap is the only obstacle between us and freedom. I'm surprised no one, not even the escape fanatics, attempts it. Of course, the escapee would find himself in a French uniform in the middle of the night in the December snow somewhere in Germany. We have no idea where we are within a hundred miles. At best, an escaped prisoner might get to the next village; even so, it would be a great adventure. The next day around noon, December 9, we are in Posen, whose picturesque houses we can see from the train station on the other side of the river. At the station they make us get off onto the icy mud of a freight platform in order to have a hot meal, the first since we left Mainz. Under the shelter of a shed we file past the window of a refectory and each man receives a bowl and a spoon, then we pass by a big caldron where the bowls are filled with a thick soup. Kiki and Nitchevo make a big hit with the station attendants. How would we react if we were told that a year from now the Polish vanguard – yes, Polish – will enter Posen!

One more nightfall, the third one, and we are almost overcome by irritation and exhaustion. Forests and fields pass by, still covered with snow, reflecting a glimmer of light in the darkness. When the train stops, some of us with a sense of humor pretend to hear wolves howling in the distance. At about 1 a.m. we suddenly stop at a little station: Strasburg. We have been traveling for about sixty hours. We were hoping they would let us stay here until morning and not make us to disembark in the middle of the night, but our hope was in vain. We have to get off with our thousands of packages. About twenty inches of snow covers the ground (I am not exaggerating), and it keeps on snowing. This is the moment they choose to gather us in groups and make a pleasant announcement: this being a border province, martial law is applied particularly rigorously here. They read us charming stipulations that mention the death penalty in every other sentence, and that we will be shot if we approach a sentry. Indeed, the country of the Borussi appears to be a delightful one.[4]

Finally, we now have to reach the camp, which is about two miles from the station. Two miles might seem like nothing, but it's an enormous distance for people who have not been outside for years, who have just traveled sixty hours on a train and are loaded like beasts of burden with everything that will provide their survival and comfort for months to come. This walk is pure torture. Von Tecklenburg leads the way and, not having anything to carry, goes like the wind. The column stretches out and some prisoners lag behind. One hears the usual protests of those who fall behind complaining to those who walk more quickly in the front. There are sudden stops and confrontations. The Germans are forced to let us take breaks at least ten times between the train station and the camp. The most we can cover at one stretch is 200 yards. Each time when we get started again, our whole body hurts, each limb, each finger. This darn dog is pulling on his chain as if he smelled a rabbit and the leash tears at my hand. Everywhere everyone is swearing. Flanking our columns, the German foot-soldiers, their overcoat collars turned up to their eyes under the stinging snow, don't say a word. We walk through the sleepy little Polish town. Our guards tell us that the inhabitants had stayed up very late hoping to see us, then gave up and went to bed. Sometimes, however, a window opens here and there. We cross a little square where a big cannon stands, probably taken from the Russians. We go down a side street, cross a bridge over a small river, and seem to be heading for the countryside. Then comes a road full of ruts and finally the gates of our barracks. We enter a courtyard covered with brightly floodlit snow and surrounded by dark, silent buildings. We drop down next to our luggage. Oh Mainz! Our dear Mainz!

Notes

1. Strasburg is a small town thirty-seven miles south of Gdansk on the Baltic Sea. At the time of Connes's captivity, Strasburg and the surrounding area were under German rule after a century of Russian domination. In 1919 the Treaty of Versailles recognized the existence of Poland as an independent country. Strasburg became Brodnica again, and Danzig became Gdansk.
2. Leipzig is located about 120 miles south of Berlin.

3. Weimar is a city about fifty miles west of Leipzig. Well known as the birthplace of the Weimar Republic (1919–33), the city was a great center of intellectual activity from 1775 to 1830.

4. Borussi was the former name of the inhabitants of eastern Prussia, roughly the area between Gdansk and the present eastern border between Poland and Russia.

5

Poland

After an hour's wait in the snow, during which we have plenty of time for gloomy thoughts, a temporary camp finally gets organized. We are led in random groups into rooms where we find beds with humid sheets and no coal with which to warm up the ice-cold air. We get into bed half-dressed. My dog shares my bed, and I am thankful for the heat he gives me as I lie shivering.

When daylight comes, we are able to see where we are, which happens to be the brick barracks of a German infantry regiment. Several rectangular buildings, two stories high, and a central building for services and the kitchens make up the main part. There is a large expanse of beaten earth, at least three times larger than the courtyard at Mainz, big enough for playing soccer. The enclosure has several barriers: walls three or four yards high, palisades, wire. Only the wire fence separates us from the shores of the Drewenz, a river that comes from Poland and forms the border between Germany and Russia for a while, then runs into the Vistula near Thorn, about forty miles below us. It makes a loop around one of the corners of the camp. In front of the walls, palisades and wire, sentries walk back and forth. They seem to be terrified of us. As soon as we approach them, they take out their weapons and if we keep going, they challenge us. They must have been given strict orders for performing their duty. They seem to consider a prisoner as a wild beast who is always ready to jump at the guard's throat. It's obviously the first time they have seen prisoners up close. Without ever attaining the calm demeanor of the good sentries at Mainz, they will soon become accustomed to us. At the moment, they patrol fiercely in the snow. Indeed, everything here is quite different from what it was in the gentle Rhenan country. And this will not be the only surprise for us. What if we were told that we will leave here accompanied to the train station by all the population with flags and applause!

Rather naturally and naively, we had imagined that as we would gradually go further eastward, toward the citadel of the Prussian Idea, we would feel the Prussian grip more heavily on our shoulders. That was a complete miscalculation. In Mainz, a Rhenan city, but a stronghold of the Empire, we were the captives of a machine that regulated the smallest details of our lives.[1] We hardly smoked a cigarette without the fact getting recorded. Here we have been dumped in the middle of an enclosure guarded by sentries and we are told to manage. There is nothing here; nothing has been prepared. To begin with there is no kitchen, no food supplies, no dining halls. The total kitchen equipment, for several hundred men, consists of two large caldrons which will turn out, during the first days, only some gruel and boiled potatoes. No canteen, no infirmary, no medication, no heating materials, no meeting rooms. During the first two long weeks we will freeze, then we will be given some peat – we are practically in Frau Sorge's country.[2] The peat is quite a problem to get to burn in the huge Prussian ceramic stoves. There is great disarray among us, who for so long have been used to a life regulated in its smallest details. The heavy luggage is arriving only slowly. The forwarding of our packages to our new residence is slow to take effect, and we go through a period of semi-starvation, not comparable in any way, however, to the first one, neither in length nor intensity. Indeed, all we are requested to do is to work it out and be willing to stay here.

The camp is administered with incredible laxity, compared with the rigidity of Mainz. The commanding colonel is an old man who walks around on wobbly legs. We rapidly conclude, of course, that he is another remnant from Sadowa. He is constantly escorted by an assisting captain who does all the work and exercises all the authority. The assistant is a real brute, always with a whip in his hand and insults and swear words on his lips. He is constantly white with fury and hatred toward us. He is a dark-haired, middle-aged, medium-sized man. This great warrior, this prisoner-eating ogre is merely a lawyer from Graudenz. I have seen him hit German soldiers. Once, when he was addressing a guard who was taking away one of our soldiers, I heard him give the order to shoot us if we approached them. The soldier was being punished by having to walk for one or two hours loaded with a heavy backpack. Some of us (who had perhaps inflicted this same punishment on one of our men) were protesting. One morning, the assistant rushed into our room before we had cleaned it, swearing that it wasn't a room but a pigsty. He left, fortunately for me, before the shock allowed me to formulate some theatrical reply. The brute's name is T***. In the future, we will get our revenge on him; we will see him taken down a peg. I imagine his anger and viciousness will have gotten the better of him. A second captain, probably a former non-commissioned officer, with white hair and a very red face is a harmless and sometimes even a funny guy. A third one, an officer in the light infantry, clean shaven in a green uniform, a Berlin attorney, is the most human and generous of the officers, the best man I ever encountered in German camps. Each of these captains is in charge of two buildings. The lieutenants are insignificant. The officers speak no French, or hardly any, and exert their authority through the intermediary of an interpreter, a poor sickly chap, probably consumptive, who is certainly the most persecuted and hounded man in the camp. We and his superiors harass him with thousands of problems, and there are times when he literally runs away from his torturers. Besides, his French is very poor and he never translates an announcement without making some blunders, which set us laughing. His forte is apparently Italian, since he used to live in Trieste, but we get our laughs when we can.[3] The guards are of very mixed origins. There are true-blood Prussians, who hate us, like T***, and Alsatians and Poles, with whom we immediately form bonds.

This country's climate is terrible, that is to say terrible for southerners and Westerners like us. The temperature got to –10 to –15°F and remained below 32°F for weeks. Snow often comes as early as December, definitely always in January and only disappears in March, at the earliest. On the window sill of the room where I ended up with my friends (right away groups were formed based on affinities, as happened in Mainz) I built a food-safe, which is at the same time an ideal icebox. Before coming here, I didn't know what a blizzard was. Now I know. There are days when roll-call is completely, unquestionably impossible outdoors and it then takes place in an immense hangar where the infantry used to drill in winter. The Drewenz River is soon covered with ice. In the courtyard we sweep the snow off a large rectangle, surround it with a little snow wall, pour buckets of water on it and have an ice rink where skaters flock. Skating is very popular in this country. The rest of the courtyard is covered by a thick layer of snow. We pile the snow parallel to the walls and palisades, and the sentries walk between them and a three-foot rampart of snow in a sort of trench. With my Nitchevo, I run wild races in all this whiteness. He chases after me and nips at my ankles while I am building a huge snowball by rolling it until it gets to be about three feet in diameter, an exercise I recommend for depressed people. These games with my canine friend are not destined to last. The little guy sleeps at the foot of my bed and in the morning jumps down barking for me to let him out to do his business in the courtyard. On January 18 – he is four and a half months old – he goes outside as usual. I will never see him again. Rumors start circulating in the camp: Nitchevo has disappeared! Everyone provides me with their opinions and advice. The 'Krauts' stole him! He went to the river and fell through a hole in the ice and drowned! He followed some Russian soldiers who were bringing a load of peat, and they ate him. I am inclined to believe this last hypothesis: he was clean and plump; the front part of him could have provided a stew, his hindquarters a nice roast, so he was likely to tempt starving people. At any rate, I never received an answer to the ad I placed in the local paper, in which I promised a reward in kind (rice and macaroni!) to anyone who would bring me news of him.

In some ways, Strasburg is better than Mainz. There is everything to be done, we do it, and once it is done, our institutions are quite equal to our former ones, and often even superior. Besides, we continue to enjoy the relaxed discipline and administrative structure we had noticed when we arrived. Everything here functions hodgepodge and as best it can. Roll-calls are made somewhat half-hazardly. Some prisoners always claim to be ill and never appear, especially when the weather is bad, so they get visited in their rooms. The buildings are not locked at night. We can go from one to the other and walk by moonlight. We soon get going again with the canteen, the libraries, study groups, and artistic and athletic circles. Life begins again, similar to the old one but now with a breath of independence. We, the Mainz alumni, are not the only ones to have populated Strasburg. Another equally large group arrived from Torgau at the same time we did, also with their traditions, plus a bitter regret for an apparently vastly superior organization.[4] Our two groups fuse but, naturally, there will always remain a little Mainz patriotism and a little Torgau loyalty. The Torgau group includes more men who have been prisoners longer and more regular service men while ours includes more younger people and men who have become officers on the battlefield, so they tend to be even more reactionary than we are. A few zealous royalists and Catholic propagandists immediately start to educate us through a series of lectures. Among the Torgau group, I myself found some excellent ex-comrades.

Obviously this region is not suffering from hunger like the West and the big cities. An agricultural region with a relatively small population, it stocks up its products and keeps a generous portion of them for its own use. The countryside is brimming with hidden food supplies. Some of them reach us, in exchange for money, through various channels. Besides, one has only to open a newspaper to realize the frustration city people feel toward peasants. We know that, in this area, the peasants are Polish and hostile to Germany. Through the canteen I order a Polish grammar and a Polish dictionary. I never receive them; they are the only books I am refused in Germany. They don't want to give us the means to communicate with the population. The Poles, tradesmen or others who come to the camp for some business, don't reveal at all what they are thinking. They are scared to death and act very official.

Soon they sell us all the firewood we want. We buy great amounts of it, chop it up ourselves, and divide it among the rooms in proportion to the number of inhabitants. A veritable work site is organized. I am among the most industrious volunteers.

Nobody had ever succeeded in escaping from Mainz but the camp at Strasburg is like a sieve. People escape all the time. During spring and summer, there will be a continuous string of escapes. The escapees never go very far, but at least they get out. One day a very correctly dressed civilian with a straw hat walks out of the gate, saluting the sentry by lifting his hat, stating that he is the dentist's assistant. He is D***, a captain of the Zouaves, a young cadet from Saint Cyr, still limping from a wound.[5] They bring him back a few days later and lock him up in one of the prison cells just above the guard house. Less than forty-eight hours later he escapes again. He demolishes the inside lock, and the outside lock had been incompletely closed by the orderly who brought him his soup. He is caught again. S***, a colonial infantry colonel, hides in one of the dirty laundry baskets when they are taken to the train station for a laundry in Graudenz. He gets out of the basket at night, onto the platform after the unpleasant hours you can imagine, and they won't catch him before he makes it to Rumania.

At the back of the courtyard a crossbeam supports a gym apparatus, forming a right angle with the wall within about four yards of it. One fine day, right at noon, two officers climb on top of it, take off running from one end and, combining the long jump and the high jump, vault over the wall. The sentry, who is walking away toward the extremity of his sector of responsibility, sees nothing. Bad luck!

The two acrobats fall practically on top of a bunch of brats who start yelling, and they are brought back almost immediately. The old colonel and Captain T****, unable to believe what they are hearing, climb onto the crossbeam to see for themselves.

One foggy evening at nightfall, a record player is playing a cheerful tune from a window of the building closest to the Drewenz. The fool of a sentry stands listening in admiration under the window. Behind his back, within a few minutes, Coupet, an aviator, and C***, an Algerian infantryman, calmly cut the fence wires and get out. Coupet had made the pliers out of some old tin cans. I wasn't astonished to read later on that when his plane crashed in the desert during the first attempt at flying non-stop from France to Dakar, he had saved the crew by fabricating an apparatus to make sea water drinkable. Unfortunately, the two escapees happen to meet a sentry on the outside and they too are taken back to prison. For if one is not punished for having escaped, one is always punished for having damaged camp equipment (if that is the case). As for the guard whose taste for music got him into trouble, Captain T*** yells a volley of insults at him and kicks his behind, then detains him until his departure for the front line, which probably won't be long.

Finally there is the great spring escape which has been in the works for months. We are digging a tunnel that starts at the chapel, more exactly the room serving as a chapel, conveniently located on the ground floor near the surrounding wall. The tunnel starts behind the altar, plunges under the wall and emerges outside at quite a distance from the line of sentries. It is propped up with boards from crates. We carry the dirt outside in our pockets and dump it here and there to avoid making suspicious mounds. Are the priests who come to say mass here aware of what's going on? Certainly. At last, all that is left to do is remove a thin layer of dirt. It will only take a few minutes and a dark night is decided upon for the operation. From 11 p.m. on those who are escaping leave at short intervals to diminish the chances of coming upon a watch patrol and, at any rate, to give time to the first ones out. Those who remain, lying in bed, strain their ears. Not before 2 a.m. at the earliest do we hear the horn of the guard, who must have heard or seen something. Lots of comings and goings, shouts in the courtyard, and soon the sounds of 'the great alarm,' which whenever it sounds requires us to go down immediately to the roll-call stations bringing supplies with us. We drag along as much as we can, on purpose, in order to gain time for the escapees. It is 4 a.m. by the time T***, who is more ready to explode than ever before, can perform the roll-call and realize that twenty-two prisoners are missing! Twenty will be brought back within four days, through the use of infantry, cavalry, bicyclists, police dogs, and even an airplane. Only two, D***, a Belgian, and a Frenchman, a captain of the 155th, whose name I forget, will never be found. They will eventually slip into Holland from where they will write us letters, discretely triumphant. This was the only successful escape in the camps where I lived for thirty months.

The normal sequel to the great escape is the great search, a formality we had never undergone in Mainz, as the camp was considered, and for good reasons, as totally impossible for a successful escape. About a week after the escape of our comrades, the great alarm sounds again in the middle of the night. Has there been another escape? No. When we get to the courtyard and our usual places for roll-call, we see an important group of military and civilian personnel present. They are the specialists who spend their lives searching camps thoroughly, one after the other. The buildings are totally evacuated. We are surrounded by a cordon of sentries, and are brought back to our lodgings room after room. The wait is long, the whole operation lasting twelve to fifteen hours. The Torgau people cite cases when it lasted a day, a day and a half, two days. Better prepared than we are, they came down equipped with folding chairs, food and books, a real camping expedition. My friends and I don't have anything much, and I am furious when I think about the delicious carp, bought the day before from the fishmonger who comes weekly from the lake area, and which I had prepared for cooking. Meanwhile, we go without dinner. Our turn finally comes to be called toward evening. We find our area occupied by officers and different-looking individuals who are obviously professional policemen. They have already started searching closets, trunks, beds, and stoves. They are probing walls, floors, ceilings. They neglect nothing, put their noses in the lentil bags, packages of old letters, and garbage cans. Then we are invited to take off all our clothes, which are examined thoroughly, including their linings. This treatment is inflicted even on the higher officers, whatever their ages. Some are asked to open their mouths and some to bend over to allow their private parts to be examined. That's the way it goes if you search, you go all the way! Needless to say, a great wave of indignation against these procedures rolls through the camp for several days. The men in charge of these unpleasant proceedings, which can give satisfaction only to police-minded souls, seem to me to perform them with the experience that practice gives and the tedium of a daily routine. They are not uselessly coarse but they don't waste any time being polite. They constitute a search machine, and we are the raw material for it. When they leave, they take away a rich booty, but many things have nonetheless escaped their investigation. By 8 p.m. I can cook my carp!

At the time of this first great search the Germans are very high and mighty. Winter and spring have been pretty bad for the Allied Forces. There was Brest-Litovsk;[6] there was the fact that Rumania was disabled even though the peace treaty was not ratified; there were the recent German attacks. On March 22, coming back from my morning outing – even with a temperature of –5°F, a jog in one's briefs and a cold shower are excellent for your health – I have the shocking task of announcing to my comrades that Paris has been bombarded by long-range guns. It's hard to believe. Then come the assaults on the Aisne department and on Flanders.[7] We are too far in the East to witness the arrival of recently captured prisoners. Only a few isolated ones are brought in, whom we feed as best we can through the same system we used at Mainz. Each time a new group of prisoners arrives, we make an appeal for supplies, and bags of beans, chunks of smoked ham and other food items pass to them through my hands.

Then a group of Portuguese prisoners arrives from the battles of Armentières.[8] At first they are not particularly cheerful because they are totally destitute of everything, except fine uniforms, but they soon begin to cheer up as we give them a warm welcome. There are twenty or twenty-five of them; all without exception are invited several times here and there. We call on our comrades for supplies, which pour in because the well-supplied people take a liking to them. The Portuguese love to eat, drink, play cards and other games. They immediately become excellent recruits for the roulette and baccarat tables. They tell spicy Portuguese jokes and right away make friends with some of the French and Belgian groups. Therefore, they are forever praising us and comparing us favorably with the British whose neighbors they were recently and who didn't even look at them or offer a piece of bread. When they left for another camp, which happened to be soon, the regrets were sincere and mutual. Let me add that we are truly grateful to these friends who came from so far to help us in the war. Our cause had so little relevance for them and yet they risked their lives for it. They didn't constitute a large force, of course, but they did what they could. And in fact, there were among them not only generous people but distinguished ones as well.

The last six months of our captivity were in no way comparable to the harshness of the preceding periods because of the liberty to walk and operate on an honor system. It had been talked about for a long time, actually forever. The honor system had worked for a short time before my arrival and had stopped almost immediately because of the problems it had caused.[9] After years of study and negotiations, in the spring of 1918 a system was finally set up which worked out, inasmuch as I was able to observe, to the satisfaction of all parties. The walk takes place weekly; the prisoner-officer gives his word of honor not to escape and not to make preparations for escaping during the walk. Therefore the necessity of watching and guarding the ones who walk disappears. One German officer and a German non-commissioned officer suffice to lead fifty or more prisoner-officers on our excursions. They walk at the head of the group, without having to pay attention to what happens behind them. It's really a walk, not an escorted transfer. In practical terms, this is how one proceeds: each officer affixes his signature to a printed form which states the above conditions. It is drawn up in German but the last paragraph stipulates that it has been translated for the individual who signs, which is a true fact. The prisoner-officer, when he goes out, turns in his card to the police post. It is given back to him when he returns and he then becomes again free to escape as much as he wants or can. This system worked to the general satisfaction during the last six months of the war and, as far as I know, caused no complaints or conflicts of any kind. Chance had it that the great spring escape I described earlier took place the very next day after the first outing and Captain T***, brutal and narrow-minded as usual, swore that we were unworthy of the favors received and took it upon himself to stop the outings after this one experience. He was soon obliged to recognize the fact that there was no connection between the two facts and had to re-establish the honor walks following an order from above. For the outings, we are divided into six groups, each one going out once a week and, at the beginning, no one misses taking advantage of the opportunity. If you haven't been locked up for over two years in a fortress without ever setting foot outside, without ever being out of the sight of an armed guard, or beyond the sound of hobnailed boots, you cannot imagine our delight when during the first outing, after skirting the little Polish town along quiet streets, we soon reach the countryside, which is

no doubt rather ordinary but appears to us equal to the most
beautiful landscape in the world. We walk around the shores of a
lake – this is already the lake district – which seems to us in no way
less beautiful than any of the 'pearls' of Italy or Switzerland. We
finally reach a little wooded area, where we stop. The German officer
in charge tells us to meet him in an hour to go back, and we scatter
all over like a bunch of schoolboys. We can, if we want, wander away
so that we can neither see nor hear another soul. Being alone is the
greatest joy of that day, which is the most wonderful day of my
captivity, even one of the most beautiful days of my life. Everybody,
of course, shows up at the meeting place. Our guide waits patiently
and pleasantly for the laggards who enjoy this pleasure to the last
moment. We walk back following another route and return home
totally different men.

The area is rather picturesque, dotted with woods and lakes. It
makes for quite a variety of itineraries, which we follow in turns,
and soon we are very familiar with the area. But our favorite route
is the first one because it soon offers new and unexpected pleasures.
With a generosity that no signed Geneva Convention imposed on it,
the camp administration soon directs most of our outings, and all
of them in the summer are toward the lake and the bathing establishment that the town garrison had built there. From then on, this is
where we halt. Those who prefer the woods go into the nearby
forest, but many prefer the cool water and for them a veritable
bathing season begins. Some anglers catch little fish and a rowboat
allows crews to have boating parties. The German officer strolls
about by himself; it's often the captain of the light infantry in a green
uniform, for whom no one can have anything but esteem. He walks
about wisely smoking his pipe. Once, one of the men who has just
swum across the lake, on the return trip shows signs of fatigue. I
swim in his direction to help by being close by, but he doesn't need
any help after all. But the captain wastes no time hopping into a boat
to go to the rescue, and I can still see his truly anguished expression.
He picks up the exhausted swimmer and brings him back. An
enterprising German soldier decides to play canteen keeper, brings
a few bottles of beer, wine and port, so that now we have a real live
cabaret by the water's edge. We could imagine ourselves by the
Marne River, except for the lack of women.[10] Only a few Polish
children come to play nearby.

The system of the honor excursions is applied with considerable
leniency in Strasburg. Some prisoners no longer want to take

advantage of the opportunity to go on the excursions. The administration can only offer the outings to those whose turn it is, but in reality, other prisoners can take their places. The German officer knows he is supposed to take along a specific number of prisoners; as long as this number is not exceeded, he doesn't worry about which individuals he has in his group. For those who want to participate in the extra outings, all they have to do is stand by the gate at the time of departure and, after the rightful claimants have passed, follow them until the official quota is reached. There are sometimes more people who want to go than there are spaces available, so there is some competition, but if a hopeful participant has put on his uniform, he rarely has to go back to his room. Usually a comrade who doesn't want to go lets another know about it, and these arrangements are respected by everyone. In practice, instead of once a week, if we want to, we end up going out about every day. As for myself, especially after the end of summer, I go out three or four times a week.

One day, our friend R*** gets lost in the woods and doesn't show up at the appointed time. His comrades let the German officer in charge that day know about it, and everyone figures wisely that R*** is big enough to find his way back to camp on his own. We return without him. In fact, as soon as he realized that he couldn't find us, he started walking back, presented himself to a policeman whom he met and who accompanied him to make sure he wouldn't have any problems due to his presence, isolated and in full daylight, on a German road. He is already there when we get back to barracks.

Generally they have us skirt the little town. Only once or twice do we cross the square where the canon is located, which we passed the night of our arrival. People seem to avoid us when we pass; nobody tries to speak with us. The Polish population, obviously terrified, avoids any situation that could be construed as showing complicity with the enemy. Besides, even though the countryside is purely Polish, there are many Germans in the town. Only the children dare approach us. We give them chocolate and cookies, fabulous treats for them. We never know whether they are Germans or Poles. Some of us have our own little fans, who always stand at specific places. Smiles and waves are exchanged with some women. In one of the outlying districts, every time we pass her street, a beautiful girl sits outside her door working on some lace. She is calm, plump and pure as a madonna. Scores of desires swarm in her direction, our hot-blooded Casanova from Mainz is in a state about her. Once in the countryside, tongues start wagging. During our free wanderings, some of us enter houses, become acquainted with the inhabitants, and so it is that many pounds of butter, many dozen eggs, even chickens find their way into the camp. There is no doubt about it; this country strongly wishes for the defeat of Germany.

Nothing forces the camp administration to organize outings for the orderlies, who, besides, are often called to town or to the country for various fatigue duties. Yet outings are organized for them, not under the honor system but accompanied by a light escort.

You will say that now we are happy, lacking nothing, that we are the kings of the shirkers in a relatively safe place from which nobody can pry us loose. This would no doubt be true if our souls weren't hurting more and more. The safety valve provided by the outings soon loses its effect. Returning to prison is all the more terrible after an escape to freedom; one wearies even of freedom in order to avoid the return. Some prisoners, systematically, refuse to go outside anymore. I feel that I am becoming bitter and unbearable. One spring day, my birthday, I make a resolution to be better, like a boy preparing for first communion. There are divisions in our mess, even though it has held together strongly through the last two years. A matter of opening and closing a window causes one of us to leave the group for a while. Fortunately, he has the good sense to come back soon. Our nerves are frayed. One day the others have to keep me from attacking a good friend whom I am about to throw down the stairs. We both stupidly insist, he on brutalizing a bird to prove that it belongs to him, and I forbidding him to do so. Quarrels explode in this way everywhere more frequently. Gambling is more intense than ever; easier contacts with the outside make for the introduction of quantities of alcohol in the camp, and drunken brawls become more numerous and more serious. Real dramas become possible if not probable; it's at that time that M*** tries to commit suicide.

It is at that moment also that a study group, composed mostly of the Torgau group members, announces (through a pompous manifest which immediately causes its signers to be nicknamed Bouvard and Pécuchet)[11] an in-depth enquiry into the new thinking brought about by war. We know perfectly well that the end of the fighting will not mean our liberation, but we are feverishly following the negotiations taking place in Bern for the internment in Switzerland, progressively and in equal numbers, of all the prisoners from both sides who have been held for more than eighteen months, starting with those who were captured the longest time ago. We are not ignorant of the fact that the Germans hold more French prisoners than the French hold Germans, but what are the exact numbers? Much speculation goes on to guess whether the exchange will include us! We are wondering if, when our time comes, enough German officers will be left to be traded for us! The agreement is indeed signed early in the fall, but the armistice does not give it time to be put into effect. Would I ever have gotten out of Germany through this system? I don't know. In the meantime, the Swiss commissions searching for sick prisoners have orders to recuperate the sickly ones with a generosity never shown until now. At the beginning of summer, a huge Special Commission arrives at our camp. At least three-fourths of the prisoners present themselves before the commission in order to get their chance to leave. Who wouldn't find himself sick with something that would justify his exit from this – I am tempted to say 'purgatory,' Thierry Sandre's own word! In vain I look for such a sickness in myself; I can't find one. Shall I tell these men that on some days I fear for my sanity; I find myself becoming raving mad? For a moment I am tempted to do so, but I resist the temptation and today I am glad I did. What stories the Swiss doctors must have heard!

July 14, 1918 is for us much sadder than the preceding one. The celebration lacks spirit. I have no heart for my athletic prowess.

The 'Spanish flu' strikes us as it strikes the rest of the world.[12] Naturally, it makes no distinction between guards and prisoners. One coughs, has teary eyes, burns with fever just as much in the police post and at the German officers' mess as in the prisoners' rooms. Some sentries look like walking corpses. There is no doubt that for the Spanish flu, all men are equal. In our room, my bed is in the middle. The three comrades on my right cough, sniffle and spit; the three on my left spit, sniffle and cough. They are furious because I refuse to imitate them. When they wake up every morning, they ask me 'Do you have it yet?' 'No I don't.' And I will not get it. I am determined not to let this stupid sickness get the better of me and I tell them all that they only imagine they are sick. They would give anything to see me cough, spit and sniffle. Alas, I know well that the sickness is not imaginary. In the room next to ours, P***, a robust guy from the Ardennes region,[13] thirty years old, gets worse. He is taken to the hospital where he dies two days later. We take him to his resting place in a tiny military cemetery, without walls, just a corner of a meadow near the little forest near the town, where a few German and Russian soldiers are already buried. Thanks to the honor system, almost everyone in the camp accompanies his body to the cemetery, even those who didn't know him, and we are far from knowing everyone. A good number of the town's inhabitants are also present. For a moment, the crowd is a curious sight, picturesque, colorful. Some ogle the women, who are startled by the first of three salvos with which, according to German custom, the dead warrior is saluted. No speeches are made, only the Polish priest of the town says a few words in French, tactful and heartfelt, words of a man of peace. The time hasn't come yet for the Poles to raise the national flag. The crowd disperses, the prisoners return to camp, but we will often put flowers on this fresh grave and will find on it flowers brought by others.

The 'Swiss-bound' leave in great numbers, all overjoyed, some a little ashamed. Our good-byes are mixed with some scorn and some envy. There is now also the hope that we too will leave one day, through the great exchange.

Time passes. The scales are beginning to tip against Germany. The Allied Forces have sagged but have not given way under the last massive blows of Ludendorff.[14] From July 15 on the situation reverses itself, slowly at first, then with increasing speed. Much earlier than they do in France, we have the sense that the end is coming, and as soon as Bulgaria capitulates early in October, we know it is certain. On October 4th or 5th they again submit us to the great search, but this time the men in charge seem to have lost faith in what they are doing. The machine continues to function through force of habit and the speed of the experience, but the reasons for its existence are in the process of disappearing and the machine is aware of it. The whole operation is over in half or even a third of the time it took last time. As winter comes, our hope grows. On our maps, the strings that mark the positions move every day closer toward Germany. During our walk outside, people, especially women, shout at us from a distance in sentences we cannot clearly understand but where the word peace is constantly repeated. Something is happening in the camps' guard detachment. Some men, especially Alsatians and Poles, are suddenly withdrawn and replaced by others thought to be more trustworthy.[15] Germany is having talks with President Wilson. Turkey, then Austria capitulate. We discover in a newspaper that the German fleet has rebelled. Germany requests and receives the conditions for an armistice on November 8. On the 9th, while I am preparing our meal, my friend de Barral rushes up from the courtyard with an amazing announcement: at the police post, the men are tearing off their insignias and their epaulettes and shouting: 'Long live the Republic!'

Notes

1. Rhenan is an adjective referring to cities or regions along the Rhine River.

2. *Frau Sorge* (*Dame Care*, in English) is the title of a naturalistic novel by Hermann Sudermann (1887). One of its themes is how to develop this poor region through the utilization of peat.

3. Trieste is a city on the Adriatic Sea, about sixty miles east of Venice across the Gulf of Trieste. The city belonged to Austria, Italy, and Yugoslavia before becoming Italian again in 1954.

4. Torgau is a city about eighty miles south of Berlin and twenty-five miles north-east of Leipzig.

5. The Zouaves were a body of infantry in the French army composed originally of Algerians and distinguished by their bravery and picturesque red oriental uniforms. Saint-Cyr, a town west of Versailles, was the location of the French military academy, an institution similar to West Point.

6. Brest-Litovsk is a Polish city on the present-day border between Poland and Belarus, about 100 miles west of Warsaw. In March 1918, Russia had been obliged to sign the treaty of Brest-Litovsk, which led to its being dismembered; most of the countries under its influence (such as Poland, the Baltic States and Rumania) passed to German rule. At the armistice in 1918, this treaty was annulled and Germany had to evacuate these areas.

7. During the spring of 1918, Germany led another wave of fierce attacks on the departments between Paris and the North Sea (Aisne, Somme and Oise) and on Flanders (the French and Belgian regions on either side of the border near the cities of Lille and Armentières). All these regions had already been battered in 1914 and 1916. The German successes were numerous and Allied losses enormous. The Germans pushed to within forty miles of Paris, which they started bombing with a powerful new canon, the Krupp cannon, nicknamed 'Big Bertha,' for Krupp's daughter.

8. Portugal had entered the war on the side of the Allies in March 1916.

9. Thierry Sandre benefited from the honor walks at the camp of Vöhrenbach as early as 1916. But the outings were cancelled apparently because one of the officers had escaped. Sandre's narrative on this event is not clear. Sandre also enjoyed outings at a bathing establishment.

10. The Marne flows into the Seine to the south-east of Paris. Connes evokes scenes similar to those painted by the Impressionist artists: men and women boating, picnicking and enjoying themselves by the river.

11. The reference is to characters in the Flaubert novel by this name (1881). Mediocre minds, they attempt ambitiously but clumsily to learn science and scientific procedures but always fail.

12. The Spanish flu pandemic (1918–19) caused an estimated 21 million deaths worldwide; there were approximately 8,500,000 war deaths.

13. The Ardennes refers to the region situated next to the Belgian border, about fifty miles north-east of Rheims.

14. General Ludendorff had already led great victories over the Allied Forces between 1914 and 1917. He launched tremendous attacks in northern France in 1918 and was successful until the Allies were able to reverse the course of the war under the supreme command of Marshal Foch.

15. The German army included soldiers from all the countries and provinces ruled by Germany, including Alsace, Lorraine, Poland, and the Baltic provinces.

6

Revolution

I was preparing our meal. I hurry downstairs but arrive too late to see anything interesting. A little group, at a certain distance from the police station, is looking in its direction. No doubt the sentry doesn't have epaulettes anymore and his shako doesn't have a rosette. Over there, in front of the hangar where roll-calls take place, another one is waving his arms about and shouting: '*Gehen sie alle nach Hause!*' (Get back into the building.) Those who witnessed the affair tell me about it. A second-class navy man from the Baltic Fleet[1] presented himself at the gate with a revolver in each hand. When he appeared, as if it was an agreed upon signal, the entire station crew hurried out throwing down the imperial insignia and saluting the Republic. And to think that this detachment had been brought in for security! Still with revolvers in hand and followed by several men, the sailor went up to the command post, where officers appear to have shown no resistance. He soon came back out, dragging them along with no epaulettes or rosettes either, and marched them to the police station. And sure enough, here comes the dictator himself, followed at a short distance by the old colonel, whose legs have never been more shaky, and at a further distance, by T***, cringing, and by the infantry captain in green, but looking white as a sheet, I might add. We gloat over the humiliation and the cowardice of T***; we feel sorry for the infantry captain. Very soon, the most senior one of us is called in to conduct an interview with the new master. J***, the clever merchant, director of Mutual Insurance in Mainz, serves as interpreter and will play an important role in the dealings with the new authorities in the camp and in town.

If you haven't witnessed, as I have, the insult inflicted upon German officers, if you haven't seen them stripped of their insignia of rank and power and dragged behind the victors, you cannot comprehend the real depth of the German revolution. Something unforgettable and irreparable has happened. The German army can never again be what it was. In some places, officers tried to resist and often they were killed, but they were only a small minority. Because the German officer has been seen meekly obeying simple privates armed with revolvers, he has forever lost the prestige that constituted the principal strength of his caste and his army.

Our new commander immediately declares to our representative that he is taking charge of the camp and instructs him to announce to us the news he brings and what our situation is going to be for the next few days. The Republic has been proclaimed in Berlin under the direction of Scheidemann and Ebert.[2] We know about the ultimatum from the Social Democrats to Wilhelm II and we aren't surprised. The armistice is going to be signed, and it includes the immediate liberation of all Allied prisoners, but it is more reasonable for us to stay put and wait for the situation to become clearer. If we tried to travel individually, we would run serious risks and add to the confusion. We are therefore asked to remain here and not attempt to escape. The watchword is that nothing has changed in the organization and the discipline of the camp. The only major change is that we have a new commander. He leaves us and goes to take care of the election of the camp's soviet,[3] which is taking place immediately. In town too they are electing a soviet. He seems to think that elections are a universal phenomenon, which is also happening at this very moment all over Europe, among the Allies as well as here. We don't believe him; victorious countries don't have revolutions.

In fact, for several days, not much seems different in the camp. We are still locked up and, without epaulettes and rosettes, the sentries continue to patrol and would fire if we tried to escape. We gather in groups and discuss the situation. On the evening of November 9, in the dining hall and by candlelight – there is no electricity – our most senior officer reads the conditions of the armistice, which a local newspaper has published. There is no doubt for us that the conditions will be accepted; Germany is at the end of its rope. This soothes our hearts and appeases, somewhat, today's worries. We are already concerned about what's going to become of us, so far away, when there is between us and France a country in the throes of a revolution. At least we know that we are not forgotten and that the power of the Allied Forces is protecting us.

The camp's flagpole, which until now held the 'carrion eater,' the Empire's black eagle on a white background, now displays a red flame fluttering in the wind.[4] A plane flies over head. As for me, this red flag bothers me as little as a flag of any color, and I can sleep peacefully in its shadow, but an incredible and comical fact is that it shocks the right-wingers among us, a proof of the solidarity of reactionaries and militarists in all countries. It's a terrible thing to have a revolution and to demote one's officers, even when they are German and we are winning the war! As a sign of protest, several rooms hang the French Tricolor from their windows. Not for long! They are told by the police post that if it is not taken down, it will be shot at. The emblems are withdrawn.

The armistice, signed on November 11, 1918, is for us a secondary event, long foreseen, anticipated, and certain, as opposed to the main event, which is the revolution. What will happen on the Rhine is determined beforehand by the conditions of the armistice and is set to go into effect at certain dates. What we are anxiously waiting for is news from Berlin, where there is still fighting. Soon newspapers, letters, and packages become rare, finally disappearing altogether. We will get to see only local newspapers, those from Danzig at best. We know that a French commission, under the command of General Dupont, has arrived in Berlin to organize the repatriation of the prisoners. Its orders will reach us some time later: stay where we are, temporarily.

The navy man from the Baltic is boasting when he announces decisively that nothing in the camp will change. At the beginning, indeed, nothing changes, but very soon the organization collapses and, after two or three weeks, the camp will be nothing more than housing for us because we have nowhere else to live and are not able to leave. A few German soldiers accept to remain at their posts. Others are leaving, one after the other, just packing up and discharging themselves. The Poles who are still here are the first to go home, then the Prussians. The garrison grows smaller every day; only the fools stay. The food services continue to function for some time, soon becoming less efficient, then practically non-existent. Fortunately, we have our reserves, and we now have access to outside resources. After a few days' interruption, the outings have been re-established. Soon, finding almost no one anymore at the police post, we start going out on our own whenever we want on the honor system. The formalities having become obsolete, we can neglect them and go in and out whenever we feel like it, at any time day or night. There are only three or four men at the police post, and usually a guard at the gate. If no one is there, we open and close the gate ourselves. Soon the gate remains wide open.

Now we wander freely around the little Polish town and are welcomed as friends and victors by everyone who is Polish. The

German minority cannot protest and even in its presence, contacts are easy. Nothing is seen around here of the invading enemy or of the disorganized back surge of the defeated troops. We only know that the war is over. Hidden food supplies appear. Order is maintained. The camp's soviet quickly dissolves as the garrison disbands. During the ten or fifteen days it lasted, it accomplished nothing except a little useless debate. It devoted itself mostly to maintaining the red banner on the flag pole. Sometimes at night practical jokers replaced the banner with the 'carrion eater,' or with the three new republican colors. The little game of flags starts. Besides the ones first mentioned, we also see the former three colors and especially the Polish eagle, white on a red background. Tragic human stupidity. In this place there are men standing behind each of these fetishes and ready to kill and to die for the flag. The town's soviet is in fact nothing but a Polish municipal council whose only occupation is snow removal and sending out security guards with a white armband. J*** attends some of its meetings. I myself am convinced that the navy man who came here to start the revolution, and who happens to be a Pole, is a fake revolutionary really concerned with preparing this area's reattachment to Poland. However, under this apparent calm, we can feel the impending drama (not the end of law and order since rural and small town populations are the least likely to fall into anarchy) but the inevitable clash between two ethnic groups. We are afraid that shooting might start and we'll be caught in the crossfire.

The center of the Polish movement is obviously located in the house of the town's young banker, on the market square next to the 'big store,' where the sales girls make us feel very welcome. All the silent intrigues and flirting which had started during our official walks through town are now blooming. Several men I know simply rent rooms in town to entertain female friends, not all of them Polish, and, forsaking the camp, settle there until our departure. The Casanova from Mainz quickly ran to the beautiful Polish madonna in the suburbs and is already at the infirmary getting treated for the results of the encounter. Invitations are pouring in from all levels of society: the nobility, the middle class and ordinary folks. When it comes to drinking, the Poles are inferior to no one, and the more we can keep up with them in that area of endeavor, the more we impress them. From a neighboring castle comes a request for a group of poker and baccarat players. They spend their nights hard at work there and are brought back exhausted the next day. There is a lot of drinking and toasting to the fall of Germany. The curious thing is that, since no one among us knows Polish and almost none of the Poles know French, it's in German that we make fun of Germany. We go in droves to the two local cafés and eat at the nearby restaurant. In these public places it is necessary to be more cautious because there are still many armed Germans remaining in town. Apart from that limitation, in the little town turned upside down, we live like kings. We now have total freedom to explore the countryside. Great quantities of rabbits, chickens, butter and eggs find their way to the camp now. The first snowfall encourages many a poacher to lay traps for hares and several of these small animals end up on a French dinner table. As for me, I wander around, sad to death in the gloomy November days. As soon as it starts freezing, I continue learning to skate everyday on a small lake. I don't feel at all like rejoicing in a café or slandering Germany while drinking myself under the table with the Poles. In the evening, I am always the first to go back to our room, where several comrades don't return much anymore. I don't know why, but during these dark hours with the war over, my heart aches more than while the war was raging. Our excellent orderly Gravisse, a Parisian worker who is a real friend, is busy making rabbit stew in a cooking pot. He is unique in his ability to transform a rabbit into a dinner in a minimum amount of time. He makes the best I have ever tasted.

What is the state of things? The German officers have gradually disappeared, without our knowing very clearly what happened to them. They have probably gone home. Only one or two young lieutenants are left. In theory, we are still in Germany and are still under the jurisdiction of the 17th Army Corps stationed in Dansk. The Polish flag has not yet been raised openly and officially. Visibly the Poles are still afraid of Germany, but five miles from us, on the other side of the former Russian border where we often go to walk, Poland is openly organizing. The occupying German authorities have disappeared. There is no possibility for Russia to take over again. Polish guards patrol the border, and if we wanted, we could easily be out of Germany within two hours. This end of November is full of painful uncertainties for us. The Dupont mission having told us once and for all to stay put, and probably having cases more urgent than ours to take care of, doesn't answer our queries anymore. As disorder increases in Berlin we are more and more afraid of being caught in fighting between Germans and Poles. What should we do? As our exasperation grows, the craziest ideas are put forward. In order to reach the Rhine, we would have to travel through a Germany fallen prey to anarchy. Wouldn't we have to beat a retreat something like that of the 'Greek ten thousand'?[5] We are seriously considering buying or somehow procuring vehicles and arms in order to be prepared to take these desperate steps if the situation warrants it. One, then two, then several men with an adventurous spirit, unable to bear inaction any longer, pack up and calmly walk past the few German soldiers still occupying the police post and head for Poland. One of them will fall ill in a Polish village, be counted as missing and reappear only after several months.

At the beginning of December a veritable epidemic of departures strikes the camp, like the Spanish flu earlier. On the 1st, twenty officers leave, on the 20th fifty leave; in all between eighty and ninety take off. People make up their minds suddenly. After watching those who leave, they walk back and forth, discuss together in little clusters, then go upstairs to pack and leave. Our perplexity is cruel. What is the wise thing to do? What are the maximum chances of making it safely to France? Is there more probability that order will be maintained or restored in Germany and in Central Europe? In this situation, individual temperaments manifest themselves very clearly: the wild rabbits leave, the domestic rabbits stay. Our kitchen mess of four, which has lasted since the summer of 1916 breaks up: two leave for Poland (Barral and Plessis) and two stay and wait (Guintrand and I). I consider that there is no risk in waiting and I put more trust in the German brand of order than in the Polish or Czechoslovakian kind, if I may express myself this way. Poland and Czechoslovakia do not exist yet.[6] There is only a caldron in which a mix of men at war with each other is brewing. The prospect of walking, most likely, 100 or 150 miles as far as Warsaw in December doesn't appeal to me at all. In fact, we will all make it to Paris more or less at the same time. On the other side of the border, our French comrades will find help from Poland in its entirety and will get to Warsaw on foot, by car, and in boats on the Vistula. They will celebrate in Warsaw and continue through Cracow, Austria and Switzerland, finally reaching France without accident. They will be joined along the way by a large group of Alsatians still in German uniforms who left the German front in Russia as soon as the debacle started. The two groups will travel together and reach our border together.

The impatient ones have barely left – good-byes were emotional because it was still risky – when the domestic rabbits seem justified by the events. We are told that a first convoy is being organized via Pillau, Koenigsberg's harbor, where ships of the Danish Red Cross are coming to take us back to France. How are they going to decide who leaves first? A majority would like the selection to be based on those who have been prisoners the longest, but since we are told peremptorily that the second and last convoy will follow the first within just a few days, we let ourselves be persuaded to accept a simple division by buildings: two buildings leave, two stay. Such is the opinion of what's left of the camp's administration and such is the opinion also of the most senior of us for whom some bear a hatred that will probably continue to rage because, in fact, we will have to wait more than three weeks to leave. Our consolation is to learn that the first detachment was storm-tossed for seven days on a small ship between Pillau and Dunkirk and that almost everybody was sick as a dog.

So we remain, only half of us now, not many more than 150, in an ever colder and darker December, in the ever more empty camp, in the little town, which is getting more and more excited while the Polish insurrection is preparing. Our men live in town more frequently. Some only return to the camp every three or four days to get their mail, although there is hardly any mail anymore, and to find out about the possibilities of departure. In order to procure money they sell their excess clothing, bed clothes, food reserves, all items that bring in quite a lot of money. Normal food products are readily available, but our rice, sugar and coffee are very much desired. We often pay visits to some Jewish second-hand dealers, and soon they start coming to the camp to solicit our offers. We see them everywhere, climbing up stairs, knocking on doors. There is no other way for us to get any real money. When we leave, the treasurer's office, still functioning, will close our accounts which are made up of our deposits and the sum paid to us in camp money at the last minute. The treasurer will give us a receipt for money to be reimbursed to us in France at 1.25 francs per mark. I am not familiar with the status of this arrangement between the two countries, but it is probably the same as other arrangements! However, the few marks we receive this way are not enough. Toward the middle of December the ever clever merchant J*** organizes an auction in the camp courtyard with the help of an appraiser. The whole town shows up to buy or just look. All day long the camp is full of Jews, tradesmen, kids, spectators and women. They haggle over our old uniforms, stoves, furniture, cooking utensils, all the impressive amount of stuff accumulated over the years by idle men. There is mud and ice, the wind is razor sharp, the most picturesque flea market I have ever seen. I sell a superb pair of blue corduroy pants I have not yet worn and that I was planning to wear during the next winter of captivity. I get fifty marks for them, which allow me to leave Germany.

Otherwise, the days are dull and depressing. When night falls and I find myself feeling so lonely in this room I could cry, I go out and walk and walk until I get so tired that I have to go back and fall asleep. What keeps me sane is my skating every day at the end of the lake. One day I sink up to my thighs into the icy water. That cools off my enthusiasm.

One evening I let Guintrand, who speaks no German, persuade me to accompany him to a Polish family's home. They invited him to come to dinner and bring a friend. They are excellent people. The father, with his big blond mustache, looks like a Prussian civil servant, which he is.[7] He says he is more at ease speaking German than Polish. He seems to me uncertain in his patriotic enthusiasm and more worried than happy about the coming events. On the contrary, the mother and six children (two big boys and four little girls, one of whom I recognize as a charming little blond who used to enjoy our chocolate bars) are quite vocal in their repudiation of Germany. They welcome us warmly: 'Poland and France have never been enemies.' Alas! That is the way it is: we are friends because we have common enemies; it is in fact the only reason we are friends. It's an old story, such as the relationship between the Scots and the French.[8] These good people give us a photo of them with an inscription on the back calling us 'their liberators.' I still have it on my desk as I am writing. In exchange, on the eve of our departure, I will bring for my little blond friend a white cat, Mizzi, which I picked up on the street one November evening and which I don't want to abandon alone in the empty barracks.

Christmas is approaching, the ever decreasing days drag on interminably; we are constantly anguished as daylight becomes shorter. The lack of light is painful to me as never before. There are cruel moments as I am washing my clothes, for instance. We can stay relatively clean, since we still have soap; no washerwoman or laundry has had any for a long time. We are beginning to lack food. Our reserves are running out. No packages arrive anymore, and I am one of those who don't have enough money to feed ourselves entirely from local resources. Have they forgotten us way out here, between Germany, still in the process of tearing itself apart, and Poland, arming itself? A hopeful sign comes, however, in the form of a food convoy of the American Red Cross, which reaches us as famine is looming. This food constituted the reserve stocks prepared for possible American prisoners.

Poland is now more or less openly in control of the town. The Polish leaders and the whole population have decided unanimously that not a single one of us will spend Christmas alone at the camp. They have arranged to invite all of us who are left, about 150 officers and fifty privates. Each family of the community, according to its means, has invited guests. There are not enough guests for all the families; some will even complain bitterly about not receiving any. I have not yet accepted an invitation. Young Mégard, the charming winner of all the 100-meter races, is very happy to recruit me to go to a neighboring castle where he has been asked to bring several comrades, and he hadn't yet found anyone who was free to go. On Christmas Eve, not a single prisoner is left in the camp; the only inhabitants of the place are a few German soldiers, fools who think, God knows why, that their duty is to stay there! From noon on the 24th, the square with the canon is a considerably busy place. The meeting point is the Polish bank, where we are introduced to our respective hosts. Guides escort those who have to go far. There isn't yet enough snow for the snow sleighs. A horse-drawn carriage picks up Mégard and me. On the seat, sumptuous fur-lined coats have been placed for us. Night is falling when we leave and, if I remember correctly, there is a crescent moon glowing when we are deposited at the foot of the steps of the Djilijevski family's home, half-castle, half-farm. What we find there are all the old European virtues, Christian, military, patriotic and rural virtues. I love and regret during that evening this world that is dying in front of the new world that is coming. But is it dying? Isn't it the most enduring of all worlds? I don't know. There is a sort of eighteenth-century fragrance to this family and its land, even though it is up to date on modern technology. Mr. de Djilijevski, robust, gray-haired, with a long mustache, did his military service in Berlin. His wife and her two daughters, one in her teens, the other still a child, all incarnate Polish charm. Two adolescent sons are present also, silent and fervent. Had they been born a few years earlier, we might have encountered them on the battlefield in German uniforms. Now they dream of becoming Polish officers. Only the oldest girl speaks French with some ease, so we must converse in German. I don't know what takes place that evening in all the homes that are entertaining French guests, but at the Djilijevski home, all I see is a charming little celebration of Christ and of the Motherland. Apparently in Poland they don't have midnight mass nor do they stuff themselves as we French do at the *réveillon* (midnight feast). The head of the family and of the household says a few prayers, a few carols are sung, homage is paid to the father and mother by the children and all the servants who come in turn to kiss their hands, and in return are all kissed and given presents found under the Christmas tree. Among the servants that night are some Russian prisoners who are treated like the others and whom Mr. de Djilijevski addresses kindly in their own language. Then each of the two young sons recites a poem in which the often-repeated name of Kosciusko[9] would be sufficient indication of its meaning in case we hadn't guessed it already from their fervor. A charmingly moderate and orderly dinner follows, regulated according to custom as to the number and nature of the dishes served, nothing like our grotesque eating binges. Very late into the night pleasant conversation continues, full of the joy of Poland's rebirth, yet tinged with anxiety about the uncertainty of the future. Finally Mégard and I ask permission to leave, as it is believed that our departure is set for that day. The carriage brings us back to the camp in the morning, although our hosts are very sorry not to be able to keep us much longer.

I believe that for a long time the French have not known any longer what patriotism and national sentiments are and they are unable to experience them anymore! To have these feelings, one has to belong to a nation that has been oppressed and cut apart by foreigners for a century or two, to live in a country where every town, village, hamlet, street and house is shared by two races, two religions and two hostile languages. The naive doctrinarians who deny the existence of a national fact should all go and visit Central Europe, on the German–Polish or German–Czech border areas or in one of the twenty regions where races interpenetrate without mixing. The national entity is an abomination but it's a reality.

Our departure does not yet take place on the 25th. Two more days will pass before our train is finally formed. On the 27th in early afternoon the last column forms at last. It is not a departure; it is a triumph. The little lieutenant who once again is the one to lead us to Koenigsberg and Pillau has only been able to gather half a dozen soldiers who still have guns, but as soon as we set foot outside the barracks, a crowd is there to escort us – a crowd such as a town of 4,000–5,000 inhabitants can provide. The Franco-Polish crowd starts walking toward the train station, carrying along the few armed Germans who are drowned in the flow. From the windows, people are waving French and Polish flags and throwing flowers. From her balcony my little blond friend, holding Mizzi the white cat in her arms and surrounded by her whole family, is waving good-bye. The German element doesn't attempt any reaction, any hostile word. It is silenced in the mass. At the station, in spite of the German officer's interdiction and the fact that a few other soldiers have come for reinforcement, all these local people take over the platforms and the tracks. There is singing, shouts of 'Long live France!' and 'Long live Poland!' I see German faces turn white as sheets. The lieutenant is on edge. It wouldn't take much to cause a drama. A shot is fired, women and children run away screaming. Fortunately it's only the gun worn on a sling by some clumsy soldier that went off, and the incident is quickly forgotten. I am afraid as long as we are here and will only be able to breathe freely when the train is finally on its way amid the last volleys of cheers. In twenty months, the Bolsheviks will be here, and Strasburg will have turned into Brodnica again.[10]

It will take forty-eight hours to cover the 160 miles or so that lie between us and Pillau, and it is not a smooth trip.[11] The German officer has warned us to cover all French and Polish emblems, if we don't want to be shot at, since we are soon out of the Polish areas and entering the heart of Prussia. It appears to me right away that order is clearly reigning here. Our train moves slowly, stopping often and is sometimes immobilized on side tracks in order to allow passage to other convoys, probably deemed more important. This delay maddens my comrades. The battalion commander, who happens to be the most senior among us, has asked me to sit with him at the center of the train to serve as interpreter. He takes me along every time we stop and has me order the station masters to get our train moving immediately. I find this pretension absurd. These technicians naturally produce their schedules and their track plans. For them, we are only a train like any other, scheduled to go before or after the others. We reply to them with absurd boasts and threats, demanding priority. Somewhere, I can't remember where, we send General Dupont in Berlin pompous telegrams to attract his attention to the obstacles placed in the way of our return. At the station, where the East–West line rolling through both Prussias meets the South–West line going toward Koenigsberg, the delay is particularly long. Through a thick layer of snow, under a yellowish sky, we make our way to the office of the military commissioner, where we use such violent language that I am ashamed. Finally, they have me telephone our protests to the 17th Army Corps in Dansk, which is still in charge of the region. The commissioner's secretary is a beautiful blond girl, and I wonder if she reads in my eyes, while I am ranting on, following orders, my homage to her beauty, my astonishment at seeing her being part of this tragi-comedy and my skepticism regarding the big words I was using. I wish I wasn't the only one to secretly enjoy the humor of that scene. I am just an interpreter and translate faithfully what both sides tell me without adding anything of my own. But several times, the official conversation once over, I mention to the official we were dealing with that I disapprove of passengers who presume to rearrange travel schedules. During these conversations, dignity is not on our side, although I try to save face a little. The commander believes we are systematically being delayed. I see the opposite point of view. How can I persuade him? In fact, not once do our protests and bragging change railroad reality. Our train will move when rail traffic allows it to proceed.

On the gloomy dawn of December 29 our train comes to a stop at the entrance to the Koenigsberg station. Why? We stand in front of a warehouse with a flag. Naturally we start passionately discussing its color: we have seen so many different ones lately! Some think it's red; others swear it is the Prussian eagle. When daylight comes, we see it bears the three horizontal colors. Therefore, Berlin's order is supreme here, in spite of the city's Hohenzollern sympathies.[12] That day I really understand the notion of errors of the senses as no psychology manual has ever made me understand it.

In the Koenigsberg train station nobody pays much attention to us. For the last month, they have seen nothing but people like us. For a while still, the train drags along the frozen waters of the Frisches Haff River, through a frozen countryside and we get to Pillau at midday. There, under the indifferent gaze of some German civil servants, we board the same Danish ship that carried our comrades to Dunkirk three weeks ago. No one cries out for joy or triumph or utters threats when we leave this miserable country. I will not recount our landing in Elsinore on the morning of December 31, nor the twelve days we spend celebrating in Denmark, when we learn that the Poles have entered Posnania.[13] I will not recount how a German ship, requisitioned in Hamburg, piloted and escorted through mine fields by the French navy finally brought us safely into Cherbourg on January 15, minus a few comrades who died in Denmark and are buried there. I will not recount this voyage because once we set foot on the bridge of the ship, we are not prisoners anymore: the Other Ordeal is over.

A third ordeal remains for us: our hearts are still in 1916 but now we have to realize that France is in 1919.

Comrades without stripes who suffered starvation and typhus in German camps, who dug for coal in Saxony's mines, who broke stones on Moroccan roads,[14] unloaded steel bars on the docks of Marseilles, transported food supplies through the Carpathian Mountains, brought ammunition to the artillery under friendly fire, fled across Siberian plains, and whose flesh everywhere has nourished the earth that was meant to nourish you, because I have dared open my mouth about our 'ordeal,' I ask your forgiveness.

July–September 1925

I wrote this seven years ago. Seven publishers have refused it. In my own eyes, it already constitutes a document, which I could critique as well as anybody. I would, however, not change a word of it.

May 1932

Notes

1. The German revolution had started with a mutiny of the fleet. Since Germany occupied the Baltic States, it had mastery over the Baltic Sea.
2. Scheidemann and Ebert were two members of the Social Democrat Party who demanded that Emperor Wilhelm II abdicate when it became obvious that Germany was losing the war. The Emperor did abdicate, the Republic was proclaimed and a new constitution was written. There was a lot of infighting among the various parties and fighting in the streets of Berlin.
3. In Russia, a soviet was a local council elected to serve the local administration.
4. The Polish flag was a horizontal white stripe above a red stripe. The German flag had three horizontal stripes (black on top, then red and gold). Under Bismarck (1871–90) the German flag was white and red with the Prussian eagle on the white section.
5. The Greek ten thousand refers to the retreat of the army of Greek mercenaries through Northern Arabia after their chief Cyrus was killed by

his brother Artaxerxes. The Greek historian Xenophon told the story in his *Anabase* (fourth century B.C.).

6. Poland and Czechoslovakia received their new borders with the Treaty of Versailles, June 28, 1919.

7. Poland, and especially the region around Strasburg, has a history of being partitioned, conquered and reconquered by Austria, Prussia and Russia for centuries. Its population has been 'Russified' and 'Germanized' with native language forbidden. Since enrollment in the conqueror's army was compulsory, great numbers of the population emigrated. The 'Polish' family described here is typically divided and confused in its loyalties.

8. The 'auld alliance' between Scotland and France against the English dates back to the fifteenth century.

9. Kosciusko was a Polish patriot who in 1794 led a great insurrection against Russia.

10. The Bolsheviks were the most extreme branch of the Russian Socialists, followers of Marx and led by Lenin and Trotsky. For several years after the Treaty of Versailles in 1919, which declared Poland an independent state, there were incessant disputes, aggressions, plebiscites, internationally backed treaties, and redrawings of Poland's borders due to its diverse ethnicities. Russia (Bolsheviks) and Poland went to war over their borders again.

11. Although the trip from Strasburg to Pillau takes the prisoners through a soon-to-be officially Polish area, it is still, has long been, and will long remain an ethnically German area. The regions east and west of the Vistula River used to constitute two provinces of Prussia.

12. Traditionally Prussia (especially East Prussia) was always more conservative than the more western provinces such as Brandenburg (the province around Berlin).

13. Posnania is a Polish province around Posen, east of Berlin.

14. The Allied Forces and the Central Powers also fought battles in Africa (in Morocco, for instance), in the Balkans, and in the Far East.

Afterword

*Marie-Claire Connes Wrage**

While teaching British and American literature at the University of Dijon in the 1930s Georges Connes participated in the municipal government as a Socialist councilman and as chair of the hospital board for Dijon. In June 1940 while an armistice between France and Germany was being negotiated, rumors spread that the Germans were approaching Dijon. Many people involved in city government fled. Connes and four other citizens volunteered to be responsible for municipal duties and to meet with the Germans in order to arrange for essential services to continue. Connes's knowledge of German helped greatly in conducting relations with the occupiers in a dignified manner. As mayor, he organized a corps of interpreters, stopped the panic evacuation of hospitals, hid the city treasury's 5,000,000 francs (in a paper bag at first), re-established essential services, translated orders, and dealt with day-to-day problems such as feeding the population and providing health services. In May 1941 when the Vichy government asked for the allegiance of the city, Connes refused and resigned as mayor. From this point on, he was a suspect because of his unwillingness to collaborate and because of his position as professor of English.

In November 1943 Connes secretly organized in his home the Liberation Committee, which was actively involved in Resistance activities and included people from all walks of life and political opinions. Arrested in January 1944 on suspicion of engaging in the Resistance movement, Connes spent three months in prison before being released because the Germans did not figure out the extent of his involvement. Shortly after his release, the Germans and the

*Marie-Claire Connes Wrage is Professor Emerita at Ohio University and is the daughter of Georges Connes.

115

French Militia realized their mistake and came to his home to arrest him but by that time Connes had slipped away and was in hiding.

When Dijon was liberated by the Allied Forces in September 1944, Connes was chosen as interim mayor of Dijon. His ability to speak English facilitated working with the Americans as they faced the post-occupation problems of refugees, reconstruction, and recriminations. He was involved in finding lodging and entertainment for the American troops during the period immediately following the end of hostilities. Connes founded the Franco-American Institute for American soldiers to learn French and for the local people to learn English. On October 22, 1944, Mayor Connes welcomed General Charles de Gaulle to Dijon. When municipal elections were held in 1945, Connes decided not to be a candidate for mayor and returned to his teaching position at the University of Dijon.

Connes was awarded an Honorary Doctor of Laws at the Centennial of the University of Buffalo in 1946. The citation read by Chancellor Samuel P. Capen described Connes as a 'soldier, savant, wise and courageous champion of the finest intellectual and social traditions of France in France's darkest hour.' Invited back as a visiting professor at Buffalo in 1947–48, Georges Connes continued to be actively engaged in research and writing until his death in 1974. Among his many friends and former students, three in particular achieved renown: Morris Bishop (1893–1973), French scholar and president of the Modern Language Association; Mary Frances Kennedy Fisher (1908–92), author of books on gastronomy;[1] and Laurence Clark Powell (1906–2001), writer and Dean of the Library School at UCLA, who helped Georges Connes publish his translation of Robert Browning's *The Ring and the Book.*

Notes

1. Mary Frances Kennedy Fisher wrote a delightful article about Georges Connes entitled 'The Oldest Man,' published in *The New Yorker,* Vol. 40 (1964) pp. 62–87.

Appendix: The Battle of Verdun

Since Georges Connes's narration begins with his capture on June 1, 1916, it is helpful to situate this event in the overall battle of Verdun, which had begun on February 21, 1916 with a violent bombardment of the French trenches. The weakly defended Douaumont Fort had been taken as early as February 25 with hardly a fight along with the wooded area of La Caillette, just a few hundred yards below in the direction of Vaux. From then on, the movements of the opposing lines became very slow. The village of Douaumont, about 600 yards from the fort was taken by the Germans on March 3. The first Mangin counter-attack took back the woods of La Caillette on April 3 and reached the outer structure of the fort on May 22 but finally failed and withdrew on the 24th, about a week before the present narrative begins. The new German offensive on June 1 overtook La Caillette which, according to Connes, seemed to have been an important victory for the Germans. Their bulletin announced the capture of seventy-five officers and 2,000 enlisted men. The Vaux Fort was pounded with 8,000 shells and capitulated on June 7, a famous episode. But the German offensive reached its limit that summer. It was concentrating all its efforts fighting the Allied attack in the Somme region. After a considerable reinforcement of the French artillery, Douaumont and Vaux were definitively taken back at the end of October and the beginning of November. La Caillette thus changed hands four times, which is far from being a record.

Bibliography

Barbusse, Henri. *Le Feu, Journal d'une Escouade*. Paris: Flammarion, 1916.

Becker, Annette. *Oubliés de la grande guerre*. Paris: Editions Noêsis, 1998.

Benda, Julien. *La Trahison des clercs*. Paris: Grasset, 1927.

Connes, Georges. *H.G. Wells Dictionary*. Dijon: Darantière, 1925.

— *Etude sur la Pensée de Wells*. Paris: Hachette, 1926.

— *Mérimée, Etudes anglo-américaines*. Champion, 1927.

— *Etat présent des Etudes Shakespeariennes*. Paris: Didier, 1932.

— *Dickens, Dombey and Son*, translation. Paris: Pléiade, 1937.

— 'The Tragedy of Romain Rolland'. *The University of Buffalo Studies* 18.3 (January 1948).

— *The Ring and the Book*. Translation. Paris: Gallimard, 1959.

Daudet, Alphonse. *Contes du Lundi*. Paris: Charpentier, 1927.

— *Tartarin de Tarascon*. Paris: Garnier, 1968.

Demarital, Georges. *Comment on mobilisa les consciences*. Paris: Edition des cahiers internationaux, 1922.

Feral, Thierry. *Préface, L'Autre Epreuve*. Paris: L'Harmattan, 2001.

Flaubert, Gustave. *Bouvard et Pécuchet*. Paris: Garnier, 1954.

Giraudoux, Jean. *Siegfried et le Limousin*. Paris: Grasset, 1922.

Ory, Pascal and J.-F. Sirinelli. *Les Intellectuels en France de L'Affaire Dreyfus à nos jours*. Paris: A. Colin, 1999.

Rolland, Romain, *Au-dessus de la Mêlée*. Paris: Ollendorf, 1915.

— *Les Précurseurs*. Paris: Albin Michel, 1971.

Sandre, Thierry, *Le Purgatoire*, Amiens: Editions Edgar Malfère, 1922.

Sudermann, Hermann. *Frau Sorge*. Berlin, 1887. English translation, *Dame Care*. New York: Holt, 1911.

Zweig, Stefan. *Die Welt von Gestern*. Stockholm: Berman-Fischer, 1944. English translation, *The World of Yesterday*. Lincoln: University of Nebraska Press, 1964.

Index

uniforms, 10, 23, 24, 25, 27n14, 41, 65, 78, 81, 87, 108
University of Buffalo, vii, viii, 116
University of Dijon, vii, viii, 116

Vauban, 38
Vaux Fort, xi, 26n1, 54
Verdun, vii, xiii, 12, 14, 22, 23, 117
Verdun Medal, 26n1

Vichy, xii
Von Tecklenburg, Captain, 44, 45, 54, 78, 80, 82

Xenophon, 106, 113n5

Wells, H.G., vii
Wilde, Oscar, 63
Wilhelm II, 60, 102, 113n2

Zweig, Stefan, xi, 6n3